PICASSO

MY GRANDFATHER

PICASSO

MY GRANDFATHER

MARINA PICASSO

In collaboration with Louis Valentin
Translated from the French
by Catherine Temerson

RIVERHEAD BOOKS

New York

RIVERHEAD BOOKS
Published by The Berkley Publishing Group
A division of Penguin Putnam Inc.
375 Hudson Street
New York, New York 10014

The author gratefully acknowledges permission to reproduce the images in the photo insert: Page 1 (both): Unknown photographer, © State Pushkin Museum of Fine Arts, Moscow; pages 2, 3 (top), 6, 9, 10 through 15: Private collections, all rights reserved; pages 3 (bottom), 7, 8: © André Villers; pages 4, 5: © RMN, Frank Raux; page 16: © Aude Monnier, Europe Media Services.

Copyright © 2001 by Marina Picasso and Éditions Denoël
Translation copyright © 2001 by Penguin Putnam Inc.
Book design by Chris Welch
Cover design by Jess Morphew
Cover typography layout © Thomas Tafuri
Cover photographs: Picasso's eyes © André Villers;
Olga Khokhlova in studio (photographer unknown)
© State Pushkin Museum of Fine Arts, Moscow

Originally published in France as *Grand-père* by Éditions Denoël.
First Riverhead hardcover edition: November 2001
First Riverhead trade paperback edition: October 2002
Riverhead trade paperback ISBN: 1-57322-953-9

Visit our website at www.penguinputam.com

The Library of Congress has catalogued the Riverhead hardcover edition as follows:

Picasso, Marina.
[Grand-père. English]
Picasso, my grandfather / Marina Picasso in collaboration with
Louis Valentin; translated from the French by Catherine Temerson.
p.   cm.
ISBN 1-57322-191-0
1. Picasso, Pablo, 1881–1973.   2. Artists—France—
Biography.   I. Valentin, Louis.   II. Title.
N6853.P5 P52613   2001   2001048376
709'.2—dc21
[B]

Printed in the United States of America

10 9 8 7 6 5 4 3 2

To my children, with all my heart

Dimitri

Flore

Florian

Gaël

May

To make a dove, you must first wring its neck.

—*Pablo Picasso*

Chapter One

There's no running away from Picasso. I know. I never succeeded. But when everything caved in, it still hadn't hit me.

It's one o'clock in the afternoon. I'm in Geneva, driving down the quai Gustave-Ador in a steady flow of traffic, taking my children, Gaël and Flore, to school. On my right is Lake Geneva and its famous geyser, the Jet d'Eau. The lake, the car, the Jet d'Eau—and suddenly I'm in the grip of a violent panic attack. My fingers contract in an unbearable

cramp. I feel a burning spasm in my chest. My heart is pounding. I'm suffocating. I'm going to die. I have just enough time
to tell the children to stay calm before I collapse with my head
on the steering wheel. I'm paralyzed. Am I going crazy?

I stop in the middle of the road. Cars speed by, almost
grazing mine, and honk at me to move on. No one stops.

After half an hour of anguish and fear, I manage to restart
the car, park it on the shoulder of the road and drag myself
over to the gasoline station a few yards away. I must call for
help. I don't want to be put away. What would happen to my
children?

"You need to undergo analysis," my physician says to me.
At this point I have nothing to lose. And so I began my analysis—an analysis that will last fourteen years.

Fourteen years of uncontrollable tears, blackouts and
screams. I writhe in pain as I inch my way back in time,
reliving the things that had destroyed me; silent, then stam-
mering, then finally expressing all the things that had been
buried deep within the little girl and adolescent and had eaten
her alive. It takes fourteen years of misery to rectify so many
years of misfortune. All because of Picasso.

PICASSO'S QUEST for the absolute entailed an implacable will to power. His brilliant oeuvre demanded human
sacrifices. He drove everyone who got near him to despair and

engulfed them. No one in my family ever managed to escape from the stranglehold of this genius. He needed blood to sign each of his paintings: my father's blood, my brother's, my mother's, my grandmother's, and mine. He needed the blood of all those who loved him—people who thought they loved a human being, whereas they really loved Picasso.

My father was born under the yoke of Picasso's tyranny, and he died from it—betrayed, disappointed, demeaned, destroyed, inexorably.

My brother Pablito, the plaything of my grandfather's sadism and indifference, committed suicide at age twenty-four by drinking a lethal dose of bleach. I found him lying in his own blood, his esophagus and larynx burned, his stomach wrecked, his heart adrift. I held his hand at La Fontonne Hospital in Antibes as he lay slowly dying. With this horrendous act he wanted to put an end to suffering and neutralize the dangers awaiting him—dangers that awaited me too, for we were the stillborn descendants of Picasso, trapped in a spiral of mocked hopes.

My grandmother Olga, humiliated, sullied, degraded by so many betrayals, ended her life paralyzed. Not once did my grandfather come to see her when she was bedridden and in distress. Yet she had given up everything for him—her country, her career, her dreams and her pride.

As for my mother, she wore the name Picasso like a badge, a badge that lifted her to the highest rungs of paranoia. In marrying my father she had married Picasso. In her delirious moments, she couldn't accept the fact that he didn't want to welcome her or give her the "grand" life she deserved. Fragile, lost and unbalanced, she had to make do with part of a meager weekly allowance, which my grandfather paid to keep his son and grandchildren under his domination and on the verge of poverty.

I wish that one day I could live without this past.

NOVEMBER 1956. It's a Thursday, and my father is leading me by the hand. He walks silently to the gate looming before us, which protects La Californie, my grandfather's house in Cannes. My brother Pablito is trailing us, hands clasped behind his back. I've just turned six, and Pablito is seven.

My father rings the bell on the metal gate. I'm afraid, as I am each time we come. We hear the sound of footsteps, then a key turning in the lock. La Californie's caretaker, an elderly Italian worn by age and servitude, appears behind the half-open gate. He looks us over and asks my father: "Monsieur Paul, do you have an appointment?"

"Yes," my father stammers. He has let go of my hand so I won't feel how moist his palm is.

"Good," the elderly caretaker replies, "I'll go see if the master can see you."

The portal closes behind him. It's raining. The scent of eucalyptus hangs in the air, from the trees with peeling bark that line the path where we are left to wait for the master's orders. Just like last Saturday, or the previous Thursday.

In the distance a dog is barking. It's bound to be Lump, my grandfather's dachshund. He likes Pablito and me. He lets us pet him. We wait endlessly. Pablito is now clinging to me both to comfort me and to feel less lonely himself. My father has finished his cigarette. He puts it out and lights another one. His fingers are stained with nicotine.

"You'd better wait in the car," he whispers as though he were afraid that someone could hear him.

"No," we answer in chorus. "We're staying with you."

Our hair is matted from the rain. We feel guilty.

Once again the key turns in the gate and the wrinkled Italian appears. He lowers his eyes. In a discouraged voice, he recites the lesson he has memorized.

"The master can't see you today. Madame Jacqueline asked me to tell you that he's working."

Even the concierge is not fooled. He's ashamed.

HOW MANY THURSDAYS have we heard those words— "The master is working," "The master is sleeping," or "The master is not here"—at the locked gate of La Californie, defended like a fortress. Occasionally, it is Jacqueline Roque, the future, devoted Madame Picasso, who delivers the sentence: "The Sun doesn't want to be disturbed."

When she doesn't refer to him as "the Sun," it is "Monseigneur" or the "Grand Maître." We don't dare show our feelings of disappointment and humiliation in front of her.

On the days when the portal is opened for us, we follow my father across the graveled courtyard up to the entrance of the house. I count each footstep like so many prayers offered on the beads of a rosary. They come to exactly sixty hesitant, guilty steps.

Inside the titan's den—Ali Baba's treasure cave—clutter reigns supreme. There are piles of paintings on paint-spattered easels, sculptures lying everywhere, crates overflowing with African masks, cardboard packing boxes, old newspapers, stretchers for unpainted canvases, tin cans, ceramic tiles, armchair feet bristling with upholsterer's tacks, musical instruments, bicycle handlebars, profiles cut out of sheet metal and, on the wall, posters for bullfights, bundles of drawings, portraits of Jacqueline, heads of bulls.

Amid this shambles, where we are made to wait once again, we feel unwanted. My father helps himself to a glass of whiskey and empties it in one gulp—no doubt to give himself composure and courage. Pablito sits down in a chair and pretends to play with a lead soldier that he's taken out of his pocket.

"Don't make noise and don't touch anything!" yells Jacqueline, who has slipped into the room. "The Sun will be coming downstairs any minute."

Esmeralda, my grandfather's goat, follows her. Esmeralda can do anything she wants—gambol through the house, test her horns against the furniture, leave her droppings on Picasso's drawings and canvases piled up in a jumble on the floor. Esmeralda is at home. We're intruders.

We hear a flurry of laughter and shouts. My grandfather makes his dramatic entrance, thundering and heroic.

I say "grandfather," but we're not allowed to call him that. It's forbidden. We're supposed to call him Pablo, like everyone else. Instead of abolishing frontiers, this "Pablo" confines us to anonymity; it creates a boundary between the inaccessible demigod and us.

"Hello, Pablo," my father says as he approaches him. "Did you sleep well?"

He's supposed to call him Pablo as well.

Pablito and I run to him and throw our arms around him. We're children. We need a grandfather.

He pats us on the head, the way one strokes the neck of a horse.

"So, Marina, what's new? Are you a good girl? And you, Pablito, how are you doing at school?"

Empty questions that don't need answers. A way of taming us whenever it suits him.

He takes us to the room where he paints—whatever room he has chosen as his studio for the day, the week or the month, before inaugurating another, as he moves wherever the house takes him, or his inspiration, or whim. Here nothing is forbidden. We're allowed to touch the brushes, draw on his notebooks, and smear paint on our faces. It amuses him.

"I'll make you a surprise," he says, laughing.

He rips a sheet of paper out of his notebook, folds it over several times incredibly fast and, magically, his powerful hands produce a little dog, a flower or a paper chicken.

"Do you like it?" he asks in his husky voice.

Pablito says nothing while I stammer, "It's . . . beautiful!"

We would like to take it home, but we're not allowed. It is the work of Picasso.

These figurines made of paper, cardboard or bits of matches, all these illusions he created like a conjurer were part of an ambition that I now find monstrous—to make us understand subconsciously that he was all-powerful and we were nothing. All he had to do was scratch a sheet of paper with his nail, cut up a piece of cardboard with scissors, spread a splotch of paint on a fold. Out came violent, pagan images that crushed us.

But I'm also convinced that Picasso felt lonely and wanted to recapture childhood. Not ours, but his own, over there in Málaga, in southern Spain, where with a single pencil stroke, he bewitched his young cousins Maria and Concha by creating imaginary creatures out of the void. That was the audience that amused him as material—like Pablito and me, raw, as-yet-undamaged material that he could manipulate according to his mood. He behaved like this toward his son Paulo from the start with his paintings of Paulo on his donkey, Paulo holding a lamb, Paulo with a slice of bread, Paulo dressed as a *torero*, Paulo dressed as a harlequin. This was before he turned him into the inadequate father of my earliest childhood.

My father, although always present when we visit La Californie, doesn't dare interrupt the special moments that we're spending with our grandfather. He paces furtively from the studio to the kitchen with a worried, feverish look in his eye. He pours himself another glass of whiskey or returns from the kitchen with a glass of wine. He is drinking too much. In a short while he'll have to confront my grandfather and ask him for money for us and my mother, money that Picasso owes him—the words pain me—for "services rendered." He is Picasso's chauffeur, paid by the week, his factotum with no life of his own, a marionette whose strings Picasso enjoys tangling, his whipping boy.

"Say, Paulo, your children are no fun. They should loosen up."

We'd better not break the spell; we'd better make sure everything goes well. For my father, and my mother who'll be asking me if everything went well, we must play along and please Picasso.

He grabs a hat lying on a chair, snatches a cape off a coat peg and drapes it over his shoulders, and jumps up and down like a disjointed puppet. Extravagant and extreme, he yells and claps his hands.

"Come on," his eyes flash. "Copy me! Play and cheer up."

We clap our hands to punctuate his clowning. My father joins in, goading his father, a cigarette stuck in the corner of his mouth, his eyes watering from the smoke.

"¡Anda, Pablo! ¡Anda, anda!"

An ovation shouted in Spanish, the language of the Picassos, the only link between the omnipotent father and the belittled son.

Galvanized, my grandfather picks up a wooden spoon and a dish towel from the table: his sword and *muleta*. With a bright, barbarous look in his eye, he performs a series of passes for us: *manoletinas, chicuelinas, verónicas* and *mariposas,* to the rhythm of my father's repeated *"Olé!"* and mine.

Pablito is silent and looks away. His face is deathly pale. Like me, he would like to belong to a normal family with a responsible father, a lenient mother, a loving grandfather. Pablito and I were not destined for such things.

How do you create an identity or acquire serenity when your grandfather takes up all the available space? And your father kowtows? And your mother will bombard you with questions after the "visit of the century" to which, of course, "no one had been kind enough to invite her"?

The east wind has chased away the clouds and a timid sun sheds a holy light into the room. My father has still not dared broach the subject of money with my grandfather. Why annoy him? He's in such a good mood.

TODAY, I CAN easily imagine the torments my father went through when he had to confront my grandfather. He had been so adulated and pampered as a child and now he hardly had any worth in Picasso's eyes. What had become of the harlequin who had posed for his father in a yellow-and-blue-checkered costume with a tulle ruffle around the neck? Do Picasso enthusiasts notice how sad the harlequin looks in the painting? How his expression begs for a bit of love? My father already knew that he would never be allowed to grow up.

As a boy, my father might still have escaped from the curse; he still had the energy to save his skin. If he didn't do it, it's because subconsciously he must have realized that in leaving Picasso, he would be amputating part of the master's work. Long before his father had clipped his wings he could not leave. As an only son he was under an obligation not to leave. He was a piece of the Picasso puzzle just like each of his paintings. He was so intent on not breaking up this puzzle that when his mother died he declined his portion of the inheritance so as not to deprive Picasso, his god.

Whatever this god said was the gospel truth, including humiliating words and insults. Once, in my presence, Picasso told my father: "It's ridiculous to use a nail file. Do what I do—file them against the corner of a wall!" I saw my father do this when I was little. It made me blush and feel sick with shame. I also saw him push away his fork and eat his fish with his hands because that's what his father did. Taking Picasso as an example was an honor.

——

GRANDFATHER HAS OPENED the bay window looking out on the garden where two miniature goats are cavorting around the tall, wet grass. Esmeralda is chained to the tail of her bronze counterpart sculpted by my grandfather; she is dodging the attacks of Lump, who is trying to nibble her legs. Yan, the old boxer who is gradually losing his eyesight, crawls up to Pablito and licks his hand.

We step outside, and I'm filled with sudden joy and feel gloriously lighthearted. For the first time since our arrival, Pablito and I are free to be real children.

That garden at La Californie, with Pablito holding my hand, is my loveliest memory of my visits to Picasso. In summer, the rosemary bushes mixed their scent with the broom, bindweed besieged the flowering mimosa branches, and clusters of poppies, buttercups and wallflowers shot up all over. Wherever you looked there was a jumble of wild grass and fragrant plants with palm trees, pine, cypress and eucalyptus trees beautifully silhouetted against the blue Mediterranean sky. Nestling in the midst of this deliberately neglected stretch of land was a population of plaster, clay and bronze sculptures—a female monkey, a skull, a pregnant woman, a bust of Picasso's mistress Marie-Thérèse Walter, a cat, an owl, ceramics and pottery, some covered with velvety patches of moss, others fresh out of the kiln. I also remember the parrot on its perch, the butterflies fluttering from flower to flower, and the pigeons, turtledoves and doves flying to their aviary under the roof whenever we mischievously tried to catch them. In the spring, we knew exactly where the violets hid. It was a secret corner of paradise that was ours alone.

It's time to leave. Grandfather is sitting at the table and we're standing next to him. In front of him are the remains of a light meal, eaten in haste while we were playing outside. We peer at a basket of dried fruit right under our noses. We haven't eaten and are famished. Grandfather notices our gaze. Smiling, he picks out a date and a fig from the basket and slices them in half with his pocketknife. He breaks open a walnut, shells it and stuffs it into the date and fig, squeezing the two with his fingers until they are coupled together.

"Come here," he says, still smiling.

We approach, shyly, eyes half closed, and open our mouths wide. Gently, almost religiously, Grandfather drops the sweets into our mouths.

It is a kind of sacrament.

If I scan my memories as far back as I can, the only mark of love I remember receiving from him was this stuffed fig and date. The only gift of himself that he ever bestowed on us.

My father has finally succeeded in speaking to his father—a long secret meeting held at the far end of the studio. This is a private discussion between the son, a six-foot-two frail colossus, and the father, a five-foot-three all-powerful gnome—between a resigned giant and an idolized monster. My grandfather digs into his pocket and takes out a wad of bills that my father seizes furtively.

"Thank you, Pablo."

The perfidious response is immediate.

"You're incapable of supporting your children. You're incapable of making a living! You're incapable of doing anything! You're second-rate and will always be second-rate. You're a waste of my time!"

In a phrase, "I'm El Rey, the King, and you're my object!" An object that he has slowly, methodically vandalized so that it will never offend him.

Later, much later, I would learn that the figs and dates stuffed with nuts that grandfather gave us each time we came for a visit were called *"mendiants,"* beggars. There are things we would be better off not knowing.

SITTING IN THE BACK of the Oldsmobile—the car that my grandfather gave to my father so he would chauffeur him around—we leave La Californie and Cannes and drive to

Golfe-Juan, where my mother is waiting for us to return. My mother, Émilienne Lotte, who took such pride in becoming Madame Picasso, has been separated from my father now for nearly six years—since I was six months old and my brother almost two. This breakup was in the nature of things. Neither my mother nor my father had a talent for happiness.

Staring into the rearview mirror, I catch the look in my father's eyes—an empty, desperate look. I never see him laugh or just be happy. When things go well at La Californie, I sometimes see him joke and get excited but it isn't natural. He does it to please Picasso, to conform to his desire, become that desire. His own desires are nonexistent. He has swept them aside once and for all and gradually allowed himself to be absorbed by a god with whom he can't identify. The image he has before him is of a monstrous father who devastates, mistreats, disdains, scorns and degrades—an insolent father who only has to sign a paper tablecloth in a restaurant to pay the bill for forty people, who boasts of being able to buy a house without needing a lawyer by handing over three paintings that he haughtily describes as "three pieces of crap smeared in the night."

My father could not create his own identity through such images. For a long time he had dreamt of becoming a motorcycle test driver. He was intoxicated by the speed and the noise, the wind in his hair, the forty-five-degree curves, and the danger at each spin of the wheels. His Norton Manx motorcycle was a source of great joy and pride. It obeyed him, conformed to his body, reared up at the slightest pressure of the accelerator. With it, he could challenge his father's sovereignty, free himself, and finally become a Picasso. But it is impossible to imagine two Picassos in the same family; it would be a crime of lèse-majesté. My grandfather wouldn't allow it.

"I command you to give up this stupidity," he told my father. "That's an order. I don't want you to kill yourself. Speed frightens me." And, once again: "I don't want to hear any more about it. You're a bourgeois anarchist as well as an incompetent."

But my father decided he wouldn't deny himself this joy. He entered himself in a professional motorcycle race, which started in Monte Carlo and zigzagged along the roads cut into the cliffs above the Mediterranean. He came in second place. This was one of the only times that my father stood up to Picasso and showed him that life did not necessarily revolve around him—one of the only times that he let his father know that he had his own dreams and his own life.

My father could never find the opening that might have allowed him to become a man. Even as a young boy, his future was already sealed. My grandfather, as a way of opposing my grandmother Olga, to whom he was no longer attracted only a few years into their marriage, vengefully set her own son against her. At first this was done with small, discreet, Machiavellian brushstrokes. When Paulo was six and trying hard to behave at the table, watched attentively by his mother, Picasso would walk in, grinning, and slip a small toy car into his hand. My father, who got the message, would look defiantly at his mother and start rolling the car around in his bowl of soup. What did a mother's disillusionment matter, or the fact that she wanted to give her only son a good upbringing? The only things that mattered were the father and his pleasure at setting his child against the wife he hated—someone my father would certainly have loved if Picasso hadn't spent his time slandering her.

The only lessons Paulo learned from his father were these: "There's no point in being good at school. It serves no purpose. At San Rafael, the school in Málaga where my parents had put me out of desperation, I was hopeless in all the subjects. That didn't prevent me from succeeding." Or else: "Keep trying to do something, but I know nothing will come of it."

THE PICASSO VIRUS to which we fell victim was subtle and nearly undetectable. It was a combination of promises not kept, abuse of power, mortification, contempt and, above all, incommunicativeness. It paralyzed my father's will, warped my mother's judgment, destroyed my grandmother's health and—in spite of the fact that children overflow with energy—made my brother and me regress to the state of infants. When this virus infected us, we were defenseless. There was no antidote. Invariably and relentlessly, our vaguest, tiniest desires were met with the terrible sentence: "Whatever you attempt, you won't come out alive!"

It was not necessarily Picasso who handed down this verdict. It was also all the people who granted my grandfather power, who glorified him, venerated him and raised him to the level of a god—experts, art historians, curators, critics, not to mention courtiers, parasites, and bootlickers who were so impressed by my grandfather's effortless ability that it fed into their fantasies. They didn't care whether my grandfather was happy or unhappy; the only thing that mattered was his power, his empire and his wealth. To them he was a showman.

For a long time, without knowing why, I had a great tenderness for vagrants. I pictured my grandfather as a vagrant living under a bridge in Paris, the city he loved. I imagined him in his old sleeping bag, dirty and destitute, but so rich in his heart and so touching. I talked to him about everything and nothing; I explained that I was his granddaughter and just wanted to love him.

For as long as I live, I'll always regret never having been able to talk to my grandfather in the way I wanted to. I wish the monstrous man that I knew were still alive. With time, I would have taught him how to become a loving grandfather like the kind man under a Paris bridge who knew how to listen to me and let me get close to him.

MY FATHER is driving us home on Route Nationale 7, which takes us back to Golfe-Juan. Below are the train tracks where the Train Bleu glides by with its tinted windows; on the left the Pont de l'Aube leading to the beach; in the distance the lighthouse of La Garoupe. At this time of day, its beacon is still timid.

Gently, Pablito has taken my hand and is holding it. In five minutes, we'll be seeing our mother again. We'd like everything to be all right.

My father parks the Oldsmobile on the shoulder of the avenue that runs along the seafront. He gets out, but before letting us out of the back seat, he religiously wipes some dust off the windshield. It is the reflex of a well-trained chauffeur. He walks slowly across the road, leading Pablito and me by the hand, and we plunge into the rue Chabrier. This is where we live, on the second floor of a modest building.

Madame Alzeari, our first-floor neighbor, has just brought down her garbage and is in front of the door.

"So, children," she says in a chirping voice, "did you have a nice day? How's your grandfather?"

She wipes her hands on the front of her apron and addresses my father.

"Monsieur Paulo, you don't look well. You should look after yourself!"

She caresses us on the head and adds: "These are very nice children you have."

We like Madame Alzeari. She gives us candies when we visit her.

We rush up the stairs, leaving our father behind. We're happy to be back home.

My mother has heard our footsteps. She's standing on the landing, wearing a tight sweater and a black leatherette miniskirt.

"I suppose once again you haven't eaten," she says cunningly. "Go into the kitchen. You'll find some leftover pasta and half an apple."

We dash inside without even saying good-bye to my father. My mother receives him in the hall. We don't want to be present for their conversation, which will turn sour, as usual. My mother takes the money he's brought and starts in on him immediately.

"What! That's all he gave you? How can you expect me to survive on this with two children? Your Picasso couldn't care less if I can't pay the gas and electric bills. He doesn't give a damn if his grandchildren don't have enough to eat. Did you tell him that Marina needs a winter coat? That your son needs a pair of shoes? Did you tell him how we live? Did you tell him?"

An unchanging litany spouted in a high-pitched, squealing, hysterical voice is followed, of course, by a merciless blow below the belt.

"I know you, you'll use what you've pocketed to pay back your debts at the café and treat your buddies to a round of drinks."

My father's replies are unjust, stormy and brutal.

"What I do is none of your business. I can understand why Pablo hates you. You're stark, raving mad."

In the kitchen, Pablito and I cling to each other at the foot of the radiator and sob silently while munching our misery apple. As usual, we feel guilty.

EVEN THOUGH all this happened years ago, I sometimes still wake up in tears when these sounds and images are resurrected magnified in my nightmares—the screams, my mother showing her claws, my father brutally pushing her away, Pablito and his tooth marks on the apple. In the background, my grandfather's piercing eyes punishing me for still being alive.

Picasso knew his son was helpless and that my mother had absolutely no means of support. Why didn't he tell his lawyers to pay a monthly allowance for his grandchildren? Even the most modest amount would have allowed my mother to establish a budget for her expenses, instead of constantly begging shop owners for credit.

It would have been too simple, too human. Picasso, who

was diabolical, knew full well what he was doing with this roundabout route; it served to make my father feel guilty and dependent and, in turn, make us dependent not on Picasso, but on his son. It was a hellish arrangement that made my father easier to crush and Picasso increasingly and forever more powerful.

The door has been slammed on my father and my mother is slumped in a chair, panting for breath. Her face is contorted and mascara is running down her cheeks.

Suddenly she sits up and beckons us to come closer. Miraculously, she's smiling at us.

"So, how was it at your grandfather's?"

It's best not to answer. It's dangerous.

"That was a question," she says insistently.

"Fine," Pablito mumbles. "It went very well."

"Did he talk about me?"

"A little bit," Pablito answers warily. "He asked how you were."

"That's it?"

"Yes, that's it."

The cross-examination is over. She knows that unlike children who like to describe everything they've seen and done in the course of the day, we won't let her extract anything from us.

But she doesn't capitulate.

"Oh," she starts in a heart-rending voice, "that bastard has decided to exclude me. With all his money, he thinks he can buy my silence, but that won't stop me from saying that he did everything he could to abuse me. You should have seen him when he saw me walk by the terrace of the Hôtel de la Plage here in Golfe-Juan. He was always running after me, telling me I was beautiful. Oh, if I'd wanted . . ."

This sort of talk is sheer madness and grandiloquence, a need to reconstruct her life—a life of her own invention.

Then, out of the blue, she forgets Picasso and tells us about meeting our father, how athletic he was and the charm he exuded. She describes the thrill she felt riding on his motorbike, arms wrapped around his waist, her senses awakened and aroused by the high speed and the exciting sensation of her body against his.

"I would have torn down mountains for him. I would have sacrificed my life."

A theatrical sigh, the pretense of a hot flash and then these hurtful words: "Oh, there's no mistaking he's the son of his monstrous father!"

The monstrous father. If only she could finally expel her gall, take revenge, tear him to bits.

"If he thinks I'm impressed with his money and his name, he's wrong. I'm as strong as he is and I'll destroy him."

A long silence and, without regard for us, she returns to her

first meeting with Picasso, overblowing his passion for her—
a passion expressed by a telling, unmistakable stare.

"When it comes to men," she says, "I'm never wrong!"

To hear her talk, my grandfather resented her for not yield-
ing to his advances. To hear her talk, he had chosen her for his
son. It was an arranged marriage.

Chapter Two

My mother always believed that being Picasso's daughter-in-law gave her a kind of divine right. She never stopped to worry about what would become of Pablito and me later in life, since a lucky star had made us Picassos, like her.

Picasso became the predominant figure in her life. Everything revolved around him; he colored all her thoughts; he was her only subject of conversation—with shopkeepers, with friends, and even with people she met in the street whom she didn't know. Being Picasso's daughter-in-law was her trophy, a special permit, an excuse for any eccentricity.

I can still remember how ashamed I felt in the summer,
when she arrived on the beach in a silver- or gold-lamé bikini,
leaning on the arm of an Adonis some fifteen years her junior. And how humiliated I was as a young teenager when she
would walk into a meeting of students and parents dressed in
a miniskirt and accompanied by a young man barely older
than I was. I felt ridiculous having to call her Mienne—short
for Émilienne—because it sounded more youthful and more
American. I also remember my fear when she started to talk,
and how my heart sank whenever she tried to explain Picasso's painting—she who had never seen so much as a catalogue or brochure of my grandfather's works.

Her way of talking varied according to the people she was
with. With someone she hardly knew she put Picasso on a
pedestal: "My father-in-law is a genius. I admire him and I
know he likes me a lot." With her more intimate acquaintances, she couldn't resist telling all: "Can you imagine, with
all his wealth, that bastard won't give us a penny."

People laughed. People always laugh when things like this
happen to others.

—

I DON'T REMEMBER my mother ever reading us bedtime
stories or taking us for rides on a merry-go-round. And yet

however pathological she might have been, she was the only person who protected us. Apart from her, no one in our family wanted us. In spite of her delusions of grandeur and her unruliness, she had a warm presence and a motherly quality. These were in her voice and her laughter, even if the laughter was often forced. She gave us a home that had all the features typical of early childhood memories—a whistling kettle, a kitchen table covered with oilcloth, a drippy faucet, a wobbly chair that you were not supposed to sit on, a vase of dry flowers, and the cocoonlike blue bedroom where Pablito and I could isolate ourselves. These are incomparable treasures when you feel like an orphan.

My mother would have been a perfectly dignified woman if she hadn't been affected by the Picasso virus. She was born into a bourgeois Protestant family from Lyons that included teachers, engineers and scientists. It was an academic, peaceful, no-nonsense family—in fact too academic, too peaceful and too no-nonsense. She left it to marry a man who owned a pottery studio in Vallauris in the South of France. With the fruit of their labor, they bought the apartment nearby in Golfe-Juan, where they lived in discord, quarreling and soon hating each other.

They divorced and, after a short breather, she met my father on the beach in Vallauris—my father, whom she would marry for better and, especially, for worse.

After separating from my father, my mother went with a lot of men—I should say adolescents, whom she preferred because they made her feel more youthful. She picked them up on the beach in summer and in bars in winter and brought them home. They dropped by the house with their long hair, flowery shirts and torn jeans. Some of them played the guitar, others drank cans of beer or whiskey straight from the bottle. My mother purred. When she wanted to be alone with them, she sent us to our room.

PABLITO AND I are lying on the bed. We've pulled the blanket over us to keep warm. Huddled against each other, we stare silently at the ceiling. We hear raised voices beyond the door.

"Come on, Philippe, play something for us!"

That's Lili's voice, our downstairs neighbor and a friend of my mother's.

We hear a high-pitched, dissonant chord on the guitar, then a falsetto, whining voice singing a Nat King Cole song: "There was a boy, a very strange, enchanted boy . . ."

"How about something less sentimental? How about some flamenco? Pablo adores flamenco!"

That voice, of course, is my mother's. "Pablo adores the guitar," she would say, "Pablo loves this," "Pablo loves that," or "That's no way to talk to Pablo's daughter-in-law!"

"I've seen it all, I know it all. I'm a Picasso!"

And they keep swigging the whiskey and guzzling the beer. There's Lili's coarse laughter and my mother's, and the laughter of the guys that Pablito and I dislike. In our hideaway we call them the "hoods."

It's seven in the morning. We have to get up and get ready for school. Our mother is still asleep.

The kitchen is a mess. The table is littered with glasses, bottles and ashtrays overflowing with cigarette butts. Without a word, we clear the table, wipe the oilcloth clean with a sponge, throw the butts and empty bottles into the garbage and put the glasses in the sink. If we want our mother to be nice, our father to smile and our grandfather to love us, we must make them forget that we're a burden.

After all, it's our fault that our father demeans himself for his weekly allowance, that grandfather often refuses to see us, and that my mother brings hoods home. If we hadn't been around, everyone could have lived in peace. Everyone could have been happy. We know that we are a burden, but Pablito and I think we might be able to bring the good guy (our father) and the bad guy (our grandfather) together and get them to make up. We call this "building happiness." It consists of cleaning house, tidying our room, washing the dishes and serving my mother breakfast in bed.

As always, whenever we make our mother's breakfast, I'm terrified as I stand on a chair and light a match to heat up the water on the old gas stove. I'm afraid of scalding myself as I pour the water into my mother's special cup. And yet we love bringing the tea to her.

We go to her room. She can barely open her eyes.

"Not now, children," she says. "I'm sick. I have to sleep."

We don't realize then that she has a drinking problem and is suffering from a hangover from the previous night. Worried, we ask what's wrong.

"It comes from the tuberculosis I had as a child," she says. Or else, "My pancreas is acting up again."

We tiptoe out of the room so she can go back to sleep and get rid of her pain. We have to go to school.

Pablito and I are at recess at our school in Golfe-Juan. The plane trees are decked in autumn colors. The other boys and girls in my kindergarten class are frolicking about, twittering and chirping like birds in an aviary. The teachers are pacing up and down the courtyard, gently trying to maintain a semblance of order and discipline. We've started a game of marbles, not the kind "for weaklings" but the real thing: You hold a marble in your fist and whip out your thumb like a spring to force your marble to strike an opponent's. We use large marbles made of gypsum or glass. Every kid for himself, no cheating allowed.

I'm one of the best in the class at this game. Squatting, tense, nearly cramped, I'm defending my honor—the honor of a champion, of "La Picasso"—and being coaxed with the accent indigenous to the South of France, redolent of thyme and garlic.

"Go on, La Pi-ca-sso! Roll the orange one!"

"La Picasso." No connection with my grandfather, who is in all the newspapers, no connection with my mother, who revels in outrageous behavior. I'm anonymous and so is Pablito. In his gray overalls, Pablito is cheering me on and picking up the marbles I've just won. We're urchins, and happy as urchins. Little orphans.

As we're counting our winnings in a corner of the playground, two older kids come and stand in front of us.

"Is it true," the first kid asks, "that you come to school with a chauffeur and bodyguard? Is it true that you're rich?"

Chauffeur, bodyguard and rich? That morning we had left the house on empty stomachs.

The second kid is short, fat and pimply; he pulls a sheet of paper covered in scribbles out of his schoolbag.

"Look," he says, waving the paper under my nose, "I can make Picassos too."

My hackles up, I give him a threatening look and challenge him, boiling with rage.

"Say that again!"

He sniggers and taunts me, "I'm as good as Picasso. It's doodling!"

I see red. Seething with anger at this dimwit who's had the

nerve to attack my grandfather, I punch him on the nose and lips. His mouth starts to bleed.

An energetic hand grabs me by the arm—it's the teacher. She shakes me and yells in my ear.

"Go stand in the corner!"

His chin quivering, Pablito cuts in, on the verge of tears.

"But Madame, he started it!"

"I don't want to get into it," says the teacher, fuming. "Both you and your sister will write out each of the sentences 'I must not fight with my schoolmates, you must not fight with your schoolmates. . . .' et cetera twenty times."

What could I have said or done then to convince people that I wasn't trying to defend Picasso, nor the pride of the Picassos, but my whole family? That love was driving me to use my fists—a love that my family didn't give me but that I yearned for, even hoping for just a friendly pat on the head, a caress, a kiss on the cheek, some sign of affection. If my grandfather's name had been Smith instead of Picasso, I would have defended the honor of my grandfather Smith. If he'd been a house painter, I would have fought for the same reason.

Seated in front of what remained of the lunch that our mother has left for us, we set to work on our punishment.

I must not fight with my schoolmates.

You must not fight with your schoolmates.

He must not fight with his schoolmates.

We haven't touched the saucepan of congealed ratatouille

and barely eaten the slice of ham, which we've carefully re-
placed in its greaseproof paper.

Our mother left us a note on the table saying she had to
go to Cannes. Why? That's none of our business.

YEARS LATER, during analysis, tears used to stream down
my face as I relived those solitary meals. Other children would
come home from school to find a welcoming household and
an attentive mother. I talked about wishing we'd had a mother
who would have made time for her children, who would have
pampered us and listened to our problems, and who would
have symbolically given us her breast, even if it were in the
form of a badly cooked meal.

Not long ago I read about a scientist who had conducted
a sad experiment. He had separated two baby mice from their
mother and put them in a labyrinth leading to two separate
enclosures. One enclosure was heated and lined with fur, the
other was cold but included a pipette from which milk
dripped. Two weeks later the mice were found dead in the
heated enclosure. The other enclosure was clean and deserted.
The milk had curdled.

Pablito and I had no such choice. The warm enclosure
lined with fur, which our mother might have offered us, was
too dependent on the Picasso enclosure that provided milk—
milk paid for at too high a price.

I remember the days when we would come home from school and open the front door in trepidation. In what state would we find our mother? Sick in bed, or wound up like a mechanical toy whose frenzied chatter and pathological discourse embarrassed us more and more with each passing day.

"I'm sure Picasso would like my décolletage," she might say, or "I'm the kind of woman Picasso is crazy about," or "If Picasso doesn't want to see me it's because of your father," and, indirectly, "because of you."

IF PABLITO AND I needed proof that my grandfather had excluded us from his life, we didn't have to look any further than his artwork. There isn't a single hint of our existence in his work, not one drawing or painting. When we were at La Californie, we would search desperately on the walls, looking for ourselves; we secretly flipped through catalogues and art books, trying to find our features in a faun, a bacchanal, or the kaleidoscope of a still life. We came across studies and paintings of Maya, Picasso's daughter with Marie-Thérèse Walter; sketches and portraits of Claude and Paloma, his children with Françoise Gilot; sketches of fishermen, his tailor, people we didn't know, dogs, cats, birds, lobsters, guitars, coffee pots, fruit bowls, pitchers, leeks. In all of it, there was not a single sketch of us, his direct heirs.

We might have offered an interesting theme, if he had ever bothered to think about our despair. Just think: Pablito and Marina chased from La Californie, Pablito with tear-filled eyes, Marina and Pablito clinging to each other. Despite the fact that we visited him at La Californie and at his château of Vauvenargues, and went to dozens of bullfights with him, to him, we were transparent.

I think we were an obstacle to Picasso's well-being. The offspring of a disappointing father and an outrageous mother, the fact that we existed disturbed his great egoism. We disrupted his genius, his painter's nirvana.

Though they were aware of our suffering, neither my father nor my mother had the courage to tell us, "There are no drawings of you, because your grandfather wants to punish us—not you—for the bickering and arguments we had when we separated. They reminded him all too vividly of his own failed relationships with his various women." Today, I would say that this "punishment" allows me to distance myself from my grandfather and loudly proclaim that there's only one creation he ever gave us, and it is dearest to me: the birth of my father.

Chapter Three

The streets of Golfe-Juan are decorated with garlands, the shop windows are glittering, the sidewalks are jammed with holiday crowds, the stores are overflowing with gifts, and carols and tinny music are flowing out of the loudspeakers nestled in the branches of the plane trees. Christmas is two days away.

When we bring my mother her cup of tea, she opens her eyes and, before going back to sleep, mumbles: "Your father called. He's going to try to stop by to give you Picasso's gift."

Picasso's gift, given jointly by my grandfather, my father

and my mother. The necessary, sacrosanct gift, worthy of the all-powerful image of the great master, chosen in one of the fashionable shops in Cannes by one of Picasso's secretaries, who doesn't know us. For me, it's usually a silk scarf from Hermès or a valuable doll from a well-known antique shop. For Pablito, a silver chain bracelet or a tiepin. Gifts that have no heart or soul. A bureaucratic chore for one of my grandfather's flunkies, who tries to cheat him a bit in each shop; it's a way of earning a Christmas bonus from the boss.

My father drops by for a quick visit. For once my mother doesn't harass him or shower him with reproaches. He puts the gifts on the table and waits religiously for Pablito and me to remove the extravagant ribbons and wrappings.

My box contains a silver pen and lead pencil, Pablito's a leather wallet with his initials.

"Once again, your grandfather has spoiled you," my father exclaims.

"These are valuable objects," my mother says. "I'll give them to you when you're older."

Back in our room Pablito and I try to amuse ourselves. Pablito is playing cowboys and Indians with his toy soldiers and I'm playing with Lélanta, a doll my grandmother Olga gave me. Lélanta is my friend in adversity. In the summer I take her to the beach or to the Îles de Lérins. She swims with me in the rocky inlets where I like to bathe, dries off in the sun and becomes my confidante. At home when dark thoughts haunt me, I pack her clothes in a little suitcase, hold her in my arms and whisper into her ear, "Come, let's go live our own life."

We run away together, but only to the end of the rue Chabrier; this gives me a little taste of freedom, but I stifle it immediately, guilty at the thought of deserting my mother and especially Pablito.

I also like to perform operations on Lélanta. I cut her belly open with a kitchen knife and empty out her stuffing. My brother helps me, directing me and offering his diagnosis.

"Surely a case of nerves," he says solemnly. "We must extract the problems that are torturing her."

CHRISTMAS, when we are little, always includes my grandmother Olga. As on Sundays, she comes by coach from Cannes, eats lunch with us and leaves before nightfall. She always brings a small Christmas tree wrapped in newspaper to keep its needles from shedding. She unwraps the tree in front of us, hangs some small ornaments and garlands on it—which she magically takes out of her bag—and sets it up in a corner of our room. Then she gives each of us a present: for Pablito, a box of soldiers and toy cars, and for me, a stuffed animal and a doll, a real one I could play with and hug without having to wash my hands.

I WILL FOREVER think of my grandmother Olga as the ideal grandmother. She was a kind of magician who had a gift for smoothing out difficulties, taming my mother's demons, boosting my father's image, and bringing us peace and harmony. We liked the fragrance of her eau de toilette, her melodious accent, her elegant gestures, her kind eyes and her respect for others.

Later, when we went to see her in the clinic where she spent the last days of her life, I never heard her say a negative word about my grandfather. All she said was that he was her husband, that he was a very great artist, and that someday we would be as great as he. When Pablito used to explain to her that he was tired of hearing people call him Picasso's *petit-fils* ("grandson" but also "small son" or "short son"), as a joke on our grandfather's height, she replied, "Right now, you're the *petit-fils* of the *grand peintre* [great or tall painter], but soon you'll be the *grand fils* of the *petit peintre.*"

She was attentive to my mother's grievances, agreed tacitly with everything she said, and offset her emotionalism with advice given in a levelheaded tone.

"Take courage, Mienne. Things will work out."

She knew how to respond to all the quandaries of life.

I was very fortunate to have had Olga as a grandmother. She was a wonderful woman and it was wrong of people to tarnish her image just to flatter Picasso's ego. I don't belong to that clan of "experts" who tear my grandmother to shreds in order to glorify Picasso's work. I don't share their cultlike attitude and servility, and when I hear them talk about Picasso's genius, I'm tempted to reply, "Yes, but *evil* genius."

Olga Khokhlova was born on June 17, 1891, in Niezin, Ukraine, to an aristocratic family. Her father was a colonel in the Imperial Army. She became passionate about dance in a milieu where it was looked down upon. As soon as she turned eighteen, she broke off with her family, joined Diaghilev's Ballets Russes and traveled with the troupe all over the world. The Great War, the Russian Revolution and her marriage to Picasso meant that she would never return to her native land.

Everyone who has written about Picasso claims that my grandmother wasn't a good dancer. But if this were true, why would Sergey Diaghilev, who was uncompromising in his choice of male and female dancers, have kept my grandmother in his corps de ballet? We know it wasn't to sleep with her, as Diaghilev was attracted to men.

I know that my grandfather had loved Olga. Fascinated by her beauty, captivated by her grace, he had wooed her in vain in Rome, Naples and Barcelona, where the Ballets Russes performed with stage sets he had designed. Rejecting the advances and impertinence of this uncouth suitor, Olga imposed a slower courtship on Picasso than he was accustomed to with his previous girlfriends. In Barcelona, he introduced her to his mother, who warned her, "No woman could ever be happy with my son Pablo." It was a futile warning: When Diaghilev and his troupe left for South America, Olga decided not to go with them. Picasso had won her heart. He gave her a proper wedding at the Russian Orthodox Church on the rue Daru in Paris.

Olga became Picasso's escort to another life. Thanks to her, he was able to settle scores (as he so liked to do) and forget his origins and upbringing in Málaga, of which he was so ashamed. Olga has been called snobbish and frivolous, but in marrying her, Picasso was also banking on what she had to offer. She would enable him to get closer to a world that he didn't know—the world of aristocratic taste, *savoir-vivre* and the appearance of belonging to high society. He bought his clothes in London, learned to drink champagne, haunted fashionable salons and lived the lifestyle of the bourgeoisie whom he had hitherto always maligned.

So who was frivolous and snobbish, Olga or Picasso?

At the end of her life, Olga Khokhlova had a stroke and her legs were paralyzed. Nevertheless she refused to be taken around in a wheelchair. For a dancer, being in a wheelchair is the ultimate punishment, a terrible humiliation. She would receive us sitting up on her bed and, so that we wouldn't see her legs, she covered them with her mink coat, a memento from the happy days when Picasso loved her.

When we went to see her in that Clinique Beausoleil where

I was born and she would die, Pablito would insist on wearing a velvet blazer and trousers that made him look like a little prince. She inspired a taste for elegance in him without having to say anything. She would ask us to sit beside her on the bed and, taking both our hands in hers, she would tell us legends in Russian and though we couldn't understand them, we found them beautiful. They were our special secrets.

My grandfather's critics often talk about Olga and her jealousy, Olga and her hysterics, Olga and her ravings—there again, no one minces words. Even Picasso himself threw her to the lions.

"Olga irritates me. I find her exasperating, stupid, annoying, frivolous," he would say.

He lacked chivalry, to say the least, in depicting himself as her victim, blackening the woman he had loved, and fomenting his son's ill will toward his mother.

And then to make matters worse, he broadcast the fact that Marie-Thérèse Walter, tired of being kept behind the scenes, turned up at Olga's, his legitimate wife, to tell her that the baby she was carrying in her arms was "the work of Picasso."

My grandmother has been called a hysteric, but consider how dishonored, humiliated and demeaned she was; it's not easy to recover from so much cruelty, baseness and disillusionment.

Broken by her many years of grief, my grandmother passed

away on February 11, 1955, with the dignity that was charac-
teristic of her. My father wanted to be alone when he at-
tended her funeral, probably because he hoped to be forgiven
for the harm he had done her.

And to tell her that he loved her, in spite of the man who
had ruined both their lives.

Chapter Four

Geneva, 1982. Frédérique, my friend who helped me when I felt like I was dying, my friend in need and now an ally in my new life, drops me off in front of the analyst's door. I'm seeing the doctor for the first time and I'm terrified. Frédérique puts her hand on my arm. "It will be fine," she says.

I get out of the car like an automaton, plunge into the entranceway of an unfamiliar building, ride the elevator and step out in front of an open door. How did I end up in this waiting room, with its impersonal furniture? I don't know. And I'm cold.

A stern-looking man is standing in front of me. I didn't see him walk in. He must be my analyst. I introduce myself. Instead of "I'm Marina Picasso," the words that come out of my mouth are, "I'm Picasso's granddaughter." I don't have an identity of my own. I am and always will be "Picasso's granddaughter."

He leads me to his office, asks me to sit down and observes me. Then he questions me. I answer in a very faint voice. After an hour of conversation punctuated by endless silences, he offers to start working with me on the basis of five sessions a week. The only condition is that I come to my appointments on my own.

I remember the dizzying trips to his office as a bitter trial. The sprawling streets, the red traffic lights ambushing me at the crossroads, the roar of the cars passing mine, my panic at having to park my car and continue on foot, and then the pavement shifting with every step, the street corners furrowed with chasms, the alarming buildings threatening to collapse on me. I feared the void and was terrified that I might be trapped in this neighborhood where I was always getting lost. It was a heroic journey for me, through all kinds of pitfalls—pedestrian crossings that had to be negotiated according to a precise rite, lines on the sidewalk that were not to be stepped on for fear of falling into a vacuum and losing my soul.

Finally, I would reach the entranceway with its ancient stonework, the elevator that jolted slightly at every floor, the metallic doors that opened with a gentle hiss, the dimly lit landing, the door with the doorbell and, over the doorbell, the discreet visiting card: "P.-A. Duvanel."

I was afraid and bathed in sweat.

I'm on the couch. Monsieur Duvanel—at first I called him Doctor—is sitting in back of me. I'm glad I don't have to look into his eyes. I'm so ashamed of myself.

I stare at the bookshelves, where I see symmetrical rows of books, a few statuettes, a photograph of the famous child psychologist Françoise Dolto, and I'm unable to utter a word. Duvanel respects my silence, with its stifled cries and suffocating tears. Then far away behind me, I hear his voice.

"That will be all for today, Madame."

The conversation has lasted twenty minutes, a silent conversation. I burst into tears.

For three months, I did nothing but cry in silence; it was a torrent of tears evacuating tons and tons of mud. My mother, my father, Picasso, and Pablito's and my grandmother's suffering were all part of that viscous, sticky, repulsive mud; my father and his servility, my grandfather eclipsed by the Picasso myth, the lost look in Pablito's eyes in the hospital, my grandmother with her legs hidden under her mink coat. They were all dead. The only survivor: my neurotic, deranged mother, a spineless puppet.

And I too am a spineless puppet, on this austere couch where I die with each word I utter.

Meanwhile I have to wait for the tangled knot of pain in my stomach to be extirpated.

"Kindly elaborate!"

The pain has to be confronted directly.

"It was at La Californie . . ."

Soon I switch to the present tense.

"I'm at La Californie—with my father. He's walking up and down—pouring himself a glass of . . ."

Suddenly I'm in a black hole. I don't know what I've just said.

"That will be all for today, Madame."

Some of these sessions take me back to the bullfights we used to go to with my grandfather. I sat next to him, terrified by the noise, the colors and the savagery of the aficionados yelling for the kill. I sided with the bull.

Before I can recover the right to live, on the analyst's couch, I must work through the kill I have been put through. How many lances pierced my skin in that arena I let myself into? How much did I butt trying to escape my dead-end life? How many *callejón* boards did I cause to fly to pieces? And all those *banderillas* that harpooned me in mid-charge, all those death blows that drew streams of blood from my burning lungs. Now I know, I was a *toro bravo*. This is what Picasso yelled when the bull would put up a heroic fight, just before the horses dragged the dead bull out of the arena to make way for another round.

I was a *toro bravo*.

When our grandmother Olga passed away, neither Pablito nor I cried. Our grief was beyond tears. Never again her smile and her reassuring words. Never again her kindness, or those delightful moments by her bedside, drinking a cup of tea. "Pablito, a drop of milk? Marina, a slice of lemon?"

A tea that I can still taste; it has the flavor of a lost paradise.

I was also fuming with anger, fuming at Picasso that he never came to ask her forgiveness as she lay in bed in pain, even though he lived very close to the nursing home where she spent the last days of her life.

Hadn't his paintbrushes reminded him of how magnificent and regal she had been when she posed for him? His egoism, heartlessness, cowardliness, barbarity—he repudiated her after he had glorified her so often in his paintings. Olga with a mantilla, Olga with a fur collar, Olga reading, Olga pensive, not to mention many other Olgas, including the Olga in an armchair that now lights up the foyer of my house—a noble, enigmatic Vesta watching over me and my children.

Yes, when that magnificent woman died, everything collapsed for Pablito and me. We were left alone with a father who came by to see us like a shooting star and a mother who was dissipating her life.

SINCE THE "PICASSO ALLOWANCE" that our mother received from our father was shrinking, she came up with the idea of suing Picasso. It was all very well for my father to turn down his mother's inheritance so the Picasso oeuvre could remain intact, but my mother saw no reason why she had to bear the brunt of his generosity.

Convinced that she was within her rights, she proclaimed loudly to anyone who would listen that she had finally succeeded in muzzling the Minotaur, the lord and master of La Californie.

Her lawsuit and gossiping merely resulted in my grandfather turning against her even more. He hired a squad of lawyers to fight her. His objective was to take us away from our mother and put us in a boarding school until we reached adulthood.

When my mother spoke about this lawsuit—and she did so constantly—it took on fantastic proportions. She made herself into a crusading heroine, a *mater dolorosa* fighting to save her children.

"Picasso isn't equipped to have you live with him," she said. "He'll put you in private schools for the wealthy."

Private schools for the wealthy—these words echoed in our minds like damnation.

Then she added, ruthlessly, "He'll separate you. You,

Pablito, you'll end up in Spain and you, Marina, in the Soviet Union, with his communists. You won't see each other anymore."

Were Spain and the Soviet Union neighboring countries? Would we be torn away from each other? We were little and practically twins; geography was like an ogre that devoured our hearts, an ogre that terrorized us.

I don't know the details of what happened, but my mother ultimately won the battle in spite of the odds stacked against her. She wanted her children and she won custody of them. The only thing she got from Picasso was the appointment of a social worker responsible for checking into our living conditions.

—

THE SOCIAL WORKER pays us a visit. We stay by our mother's side, watching this intruding woman's every move. She opens the refrigerator to see what it contains, checks our notebooks, inspects our wardrobe and quizzes us on our life with our mother. We are lawbreakers subjected to a court ruling.

"What did you eat for lunch? At what time did you go to bed?"

We lower our eyes; we're afraid of answering.

The social worker's name is Madame Boeuf. She's a pretty

redhead. Occasionally she smiles at us, and on one occasion she gave me some candy.

"Why do you come and ruin all our Thursdays?" I say to her, tearfully.

She crouches down in front of me, looks into my eyes and says: "I cross my heart, Marina dear, I won't come and ruin your Thursdays anymore."

We become friends and I find I can explain a lot of things to her.

"Madame Boeuf, I like Bécassine," I say, referring to the storybook character whose name means "silly goose."

She looks at me wide-eyed but lets me speak.

"You know, Bécassine is a simple person. She's not stupid though. She even knows a lot, but she's usually unlucky. She tries to go mountain climbing and she always falls. She doesn't do it to make people laugh, she just can't climb up the mountain. If people would listen to Bécassine, they would realize that she's full of potential. She would be intelligent if she wasn't asked to climb up those horrible mountains . . ."

Then I fall silent. Grown-ups don't really understand life.

—

THURSDAY WAS ALSO the day school was not in session; this was the only day we felt free. On that day, we would get up very early, jump into our clothes and run out to join our pals in the street. Sometimes, as we ran by, Madame Alzeari or Lili, the downstairs neighbor, would stop us and give us a slice of cake or a piece of candy. They knew our mother had no desire to bake cakes and even less desire to squander money on candies. We would thank them with our mouths full. Then we would bicycle down to the beach, followed by a bunch of kids from the rue Chabrier.

My bicycle must have been the equivalent, for me, of the Norton Manx motorbike for my father. I would jump on and, standing erect on the pedals, zip straight down to the landing pier in Golfe-Juan harbor. I brake at the very last second with a screech of tires, two inches away from the end of the landing. Since we only had one bike for the two of us, Pablito would sometimes borrow it from me when he wanted to pedal cautiously along the waterfront. I was more of a daredevil than he.

I also loved to jump into the sea. I could only dog-paddle, but I did it extremely well. I enjoyed swimming out to the open sea, beyond the area marked for swimming by the rubber rings. This made me feel free from my mother and father and—small revenge—from Picasso, who was afraid when he couldn't touch bottom.

I remember too the small boat that we appropriated and made into an ocean liner. It was an old sea- and sand-worn dinghy, a wreck abandoned to its fate by fishermen. With a few boards, four nails, tar and a coat of paint—unearthed God knows where—my friends and I patched it up so it could float. We would take turns climbing on board, two or three at a time, rarely more, row like galley slaves, bale out like maniacs and swim back after sinking a few yards from the shore. The odyssey itself was unimportant. What counted was the dream—the dream of going very far away, beyond the horizon, with my travel companions Pablito and Alain, a friend of ours who was as mixed-up as we were.

MY FATHER LEFT a message saying he would try to stop by. For three months he'd been trying to stop by. Madame Boeuf said this was nothing to worry about; we had to wait for things to get better.

It was all very well to wait for things to get better, but my mother, as she put it, couldn't make ends meet. She was greeted coldly by the butcher and the grocer when she asked them if she could put off paying them. Of course, we had to listen to her everlasting complaints.

"I bleed myself to bring you up while your father is out having a good time. He couldn't care less that I'm worried. And Picasso couldn't care less if I get sick. . . ."

We were brought up on the words "sick" and "worried." That's what life must have been all about.

The lean times stretched out day after day, week after week, month after month. We had to be careful about everything.

"Pablito, take care of your clothes. Marina, don't ruin your shoes. For dessert, you can split a banana."

Irregular meals, unbuttered toast dipped in warm milk, scrambled eggs with tomato pulp, pasta with meager sauces, poor man's rice.

When you're a child, skipping a meal is not important so long as you know you're loved. Much more serious is being asphyxiated by a mother's endless, solemn and dogmatic discourses. Our mother used to dispense her knowledge like a tyrant, between two mouthfuls. She would interrupt us, speak for us, and inflict her theories on everything.

"Melon and strawberries are the best fruits."

"I love pink. Picasso used to tell me that it suited my complexion."

"I only like short skirts."

"I only like big breasts."

"Picasso also likes short skirts . . . and big breasts . . . and that Algerian war that's dragging out. Not surprising with that National Liberation Front that Picasso supports."

A string of pathetic inanities that used to spoil the moments we spent together.

And yet when spring comes around, we are happy when we get up from the table, with June heralding vacation, the beach, the bike, the dinghy, the pals. Our mother is delighted also; she looks forward to lying on the beach again in her bikini with her bunch of hoods.

We are happy in spite of her—in spite of everything.

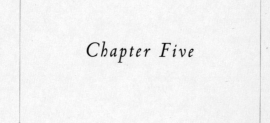

Chapter Five

The telephone rings in the night. Jolted awake, Pablito and I hold our breath. We know it's our father. He must be calling from a bar as usual. Three, four rings, then silence. My mother has picked up the phone in her room.

"Do you think he wants to see us?" Pablito whispers.

I don't say anything. I'd like it to be true.

We're up early in the morning and busy tidying the kitchen; there are dishes to be washed, the floor has to be mopped, and laundry has to be put out to dry on the balcony.

Then we have to prepare our mother's breakfast—lay out

the cup, the teapot and the sugar on a tray. No, no sugar; sugar is fattening. We look at the clock. It's nine. We have two hours to kill before waking her up. So we wait, not daring to move.

It was our father who had called.

"He remembers that he has children," my mother grumbles. "He said he would come by and pick you up."

"When?"

"At one o'clock. Downstairs."

Downstairs, because he is no longer allowed to come up. We can't show him our room, the fortified castle Pablito built in a shoe box, our school notebooks or the drawings we've put up on the walls.

Our father is an undesirable. We can't share our child's world with him ever again.

MY FATHER TAKES us to La Californie, where we go through the old ritual: the wait in front of the gate, the old concierge's footsteps, the key in the lock and the cutting words: "You have an appointment?"

We cross the graveled courtyard up to the front steps; there we're met by the watchdog, Jacqueline Roque.

"Monseigneur is taking his shower. In the meantime, go play in the garden."

Her tone of voice is gruff and arrogant. She's the lord and master of the place. We must obey.

Pablito and I walk hand in hand and are followed by

Lump, the dachshund. We don't dare run or talk to each other. Monseigneur is taking his shower. We must not disturb that solemn moment.

Our father is right behind us, a cigarette in his mouth. Stooped, he walks among the statues surrounded by wild grass. Casually, he gathers a sprig of lavender that he brings up to his nostrils. Does its scent remind him of his early childhood? Of a time when Picasso still respected him?

I abandon Pablito to join my father and slip my hand into his. I love him. He's my father.

We're in the studio. My grandfather welcomes us in his underpants, loose cotton underpants, his overflowing attributes visible—an affront to me, as an eight-year-old girl, or later as a seventeen-year-old, whom he will receive in the same way at the end of his life.

Was it an affront or a provocation? I think he just wasn't embarrassed to show himself this way at seventy-seven, in front of me, the cook or the young cleaning woman. His sexual organ was like his paintbrushes, the fish bones piled up in his plate, Esmeralda's droppings scattered here and there, or the piles of rusting tin cans heaped up on the ground. Cock, paintbrushes, fish bones, droppings, rusted cans—these were all part of his work, part of the Picasso volume that everyone had to accept. Even if it was shocking.

The date, the fig, the walnut, consecrated by his fingers, a huge roar of laughter, and then a lesson in wisdom, absurd and irrational.

"Children, you should know that one can do without everything and live very well—without shoes, clothes, even food. Look at me, I don't need anything."

Pablito and I blush to the roots of our hair. Had our mother sent him a letter of complaint? Would he refuse to give my father his allowance? Once again, we feel guilty for existing.

Yet it's true he doesn't need anything, with his torn sailor's jersey, his ill-adjusted underpants, his worn espadrilles. What do we have to complain about? Our grandfather is like us. A pauper. The only difference is that he has a pile of money, whereas we'll be eating pasta again tonight.

"The important thing," he adds, radiant, "is to do what you feel like doing."

The statement hits my father like a slap in the face. He lowers his eyes and stammers.

"Pablo, I brought back the paintings you wanted from Paris. They're in the car."

Sidestepping, evasiveness and fear—once again my father is afraid of displeasing the powerful Minotaur, the deus ex machina of his pitiful destiny.

Grandfather does not react. He merely smiles.

"Paulo," he says finally, "next Sunday, Dominguín will be fighting a bull in Arles. You'll come with me."

And then, turning toward us, he adds: "If you want, bring Pablito and Marina. After all, they have Spanish blood."

The visit is over. Pablito and I gratefully thank Grandfather for the wonderful day. He leans down toward us, accepts

our kisses and exclaims with a laugh: *"¡Hasta la vista, muchachos!
¡A domingo próximo!"*

We walk toward the metal gate, where my father is un-
loading the paintings that were inside the trunk of the
Oldsmobile. He brings them into the house and asks us to
wait quietly.

He returns with a spring in his step and a happy expression. Evidently, my grandfather had been charitable—not
with his heart but with his money.

That evening we eat pizza at Da Luigi, a trattoria in the
Golfe-Juan harbor. A slice of luxury.

⟐

DURING THE BEST VISITS to La Californie, my father
was relaxed and made my grandfather happy. They would
speak of Spain, of cousins who still lived there, of travel
plans, and they held each other in a cordial *abrazo*. Pablito and
I would hold our breath, afraid of dispelling the happiness.

When we were little, Pablito and I were part of what my
grandfather called "the gang of children," which included
Paloma and Claude, Françoise Gilot's children, and Catherine Hutin, Jacqueline Roque's daughter. As part of this gang,
Pablito and I felt freer. We were all about the same age, give
or take two or three years. We were all mischievous and re-
bellious and thrived in the anarchical disorderliness of La
Californie. We played hopscotch on the mosaic in the foyer,
tag among the trees and statues in the garden, hide-and-seek

amidst the junk in the studio. We raced boisterously up the stairs to the upper floor. The rumpus, rowdiness and cacophony were encouraged by Picasso's cries of joy—father to some, grandfather to others, playmate to all.

Those moments seemed magical to me. We were finally recognized and accepted. When we drew lots for a game of blindman's buff and it was my turn to be blindfolded, I was so unwilling to lose sight momentarily of the miracle that I used to yell, "Leave me alone, I don't want to not see."

Not want to not see—two negatives equal an affirmation. I wanted to collect every crumb of an exceptional happiness.

This was the blessed time when Paloma and Claude were still allowed at La Californie, before their mother decided to unlock the door to the cage where Picasso had kept her for too long. This was the blessed time when Pablito and I had not yet witnessed the violent clashes between our mother and father. The blessed time when we were able to be just children.

Sometimes we would all spend the night together in a room converted into a dormitory. But it was never more than one night. Our presence disrupted Picasso's work and disturbed Jacqueline Roque. She wanted to be alone with her Monseigneur, in the golden prison she was building around him.

And then there were the visits where Pablito and I didn't dare give the slightest sign of our presence—the visits in which my father was subjected to reproaches in front of us. During these visits, as a form of escapism, I concentrated my thoughts on the sea, the sun, the beach, my friends and the old dinghy.

I made up an imaginary fisherman father who would take me out on the open sea every day and sell his daily catch at the market. I made up an imaginary mother who would be ready to clean houses rather than be dependent on Picasso—and a Picasso who would be a real grandfather. I made up parents who were not part of the world that had been chosen for me.

I also recall the Sundays when Catherine Hutin would tell us about the school where her mother enrolled her as a boarder so Monseigneur would not be disturbed. Since she knew nothing else of life, she would conduct a mock class for us in her little room. An inflexible teacher with a wheedling smile, she would hit our fingers with a ruler. Perhaps inflicting this punishment on us was her way of relieving her resentment toward Picasso, who did not want her to live at La Californie.

There was also the day when, to my amazement, I saw my grandfather look sad for the first time. I wanted to check how many minutes were left before Jacqueline Roque—now Madame Picasso—informed us that the visit was over, and without thinking I had consulted my wristwatch, a very recent gift from my mother in a burst of generosity. Grandfather suddenly had a pained look in his eye.

"Are you bored?" he asked me.

For the first time, my grandfather was distressed; he seemed genuinely hurt, like a real grandfather.

I didn't want to break the spell, so I didn't answer. I was afraid that the Picasso who was inconvenienced by us would resurface and drive away the flash of affection—a moment still engraved in my memory.

—

I'M BACK in Geneva on my torture couch, holding on to my last hope. I'm crying. I only know how to cry and feel guilty.

"Why couldn't I see?"

Behind me, I hear the analyst's voice.

"Couldn't see? Be clear."

I'm silent. How can I express the emotions that are battling within me? Impressions of regret, love and resentment.

I'm in pain.

Why didn't I understand that Picasso was indifferent to everything outside his work? His life didn't center on Pablito or me, my father, my mother, my grandmother Olga, or the women whose deaths he brought about. There was only one thing that mattered to him: painting and nothing else. In order to create, he had to destroy everything that got in the way of his creation.

A painting, he told Christian Zervos, founder of the journal *Cahiers d'Art*, is "a series of additions. For me, a painting is a series of destructions."

And here we were, longing for a glance. How were we to know that he had to destroy *us* as well.

"Monseigneur isn't here."

Monseigneur couldn't be there—not for us, or his other victims. We were mere refuse for his art.

"That will be all for today, Madame."

Chapter Six

A few years after my grandfather bought La Californie, he bought another house, in Vauvenargues, a village about ten miles north of Arles. The house had four towers and forty windows. I know because I counted them, with the mistral wind blowing through my hair, and my eyes squinting against the holiday sun. This is where we went when we accompanied Grandfather and Father to the grape harvest bullfights in Arles. We sometimes went there without Picasso and, to scare us, our father would tell us that it was haunted by the ghost of its first owner, Luc de Clapiers, Marquis de Vauvenargues.

As promised, our grandfather takes us to Arles. There we hear the cries of vendors running through rows of spectators to hawk cushions—red, orange, purple, blue cushions that are being snapped up by people who want to be more comfortably seated on the stone steps of the Roman amphitheater. Other merchants are selling ice cream, beignets, peanuts, drinks. The crowd is noisy, swarming and buzzing like bees, excited, fanatical; they have to see blood flow.

In the arena, the *peones,* the matadors' helpers, are leveling the freshly watered-down ocher sand. It is the hour when the sun maps out corners of shade and light where the bull will choose to fight. And there, in the first row, are my grandfather, my father and Pablito. Three generations of Spaniards driven by the same passion—that of defying life and challenging death.

At the top of the steps, the heralds blow their trumpets. This is the signal for the *alguacils,* two horsemen dressed in black in a style dating back to the reign of Philip II, to gallop across the ring and stop in front of the president's box. He gestures, giving them the privilege of opening the bullfight. The crowd stands on the steps, cheering them.

The Picasso clan—Pablo, Paulo, Pablito—hasn't moved a muscle. Picassos don't mix with the jubilant mob.

The procession begins, to the sound of brass instruments.

Three matadors emerge from a passageway to the horses' enclosure and walk into the arena. With ceremonial capes draped over their left arms, they take small steps, chins raised and chests thrust out.

The gold on their clothes sparkles in the sunlight.

Picasso's eyes are burning feverishly. Mentally, he and Paulo will be fighting too. They smile, exchange looks and pay homage to one another.

"*¿Qué tal, Pablo?*"

"*¡Muy bien, hijo!* Luis Miguel promises a good fight."

Luis Miguel is Domínguín, the matador the aficionados have come specially to honor today. Domínguín, the man who has fought, speared and killed more than two thousand bulls in his career. Luis Miguel Domínguín, whom the Picassos, Pablito included, joined that morning at the Hôtel Nord Pinus to watch while he put on his glittering attire—a favor reserved for family and close friends—before he secluded himself to implore the help of the Virgin and Saint Veronica.

"A good fight before being gored," adds Pablito with pride, looking into my eyes.

Death with perforated guts and spurting blood.

Like my brother Pablito's death. Much later. In a completely different arena.

Behind the matadors—with Domínguín walking in the center—are the twelve *banderilleros* and eight *picadores*, by order of seniority, on their caparisoned horses, miserable nags with crooked legs and lowered ears.

My eyes meet Picasso's. He averts his gaze. My presence disturbs him.

"Why do you cry over the fate of those horses?" he asked me one day. "They're old and only good for the butcher shop."

The parade is over. The *picadores* have left the arena. The attendants are smoothing the sand stirred up by the horses' hooves. The matadors and their *cuadrillas,* or teams, have returned to the *callejón,* the passageway that runs the length of the arena and serves as their sanctuary. While waiting to fight, they have unfolded their heavy ceremonial capes and draped them over the fence protecting the first row of seats. Dominguín has sent his to Jacqueline Picasso; she is sitting in the second row next to Jean Cocteau, who has made the trip specially from Saint-Jean-Cap-Ferrat. Dominguín then goes up to the barrier in front of the first row of seats and selects a combat cape that is cherry red on the outside and yellow on the inside.

Picasso's eagle eye is recording every gesture. Tonight or tomorrow they will be reproduced on a canvas or a dish or, immediately after the fight, in that notebook with which he never parts. My father avoids speaking to him. He knows that this transcendent moment must not be disrupted; it is like the moment just before the kill when Dominguín will be cradled between the bull's horns.

Pablito also respects this mystery. His chin propped between his fists, he is staring at his grandfather. At this very
moment, lost in their thoughts, they resemble each other so
much.

And so does Dominguín, who, behind his *burladero*—the
wooden screen in the arena that provides the matador with a
refuge—is bracing himself to face fear.

The bullpen door releases its first bull, and a tidal wave of
violence sweeps through the ring; the bull churns the arena's
sand furiously with his hooves and collides head-on with
the boards of the *callejón;* he catches his breath, foams at the
mouth and rears up.

He's alone with his overwhelming rage. Having to save his
skin alone—just like Picasso when he burns with the desire
to attain the absolute by painting a canvas.

One of the *banderilleros* walks toward the bull, taunts him
with his cape and forces him to charge. Behind his shelter,
Dominguín studies his leaps and his butting movements; he
evaluates the bull's power, shortcomings and boldness. His
face twitches.

It's his turn now to challenge the animal. He walks into the
arena with small, sliding steps. The bull stands firm. His
muscles are tense and quivering. Dominguín provokes him
head on. He remains motionless. The bull swoops down on
him and is engulfed in the folds of the cape. His right horn
grazes Dominguín's chest. Beast and man are fused. Without

flinching, the man performs his moves: *verónicas, manoletinas,* dangerous, perfect, faultless *parones.*

"*¡Olé!*"

"*¡Anda!*"

The crowd in the arena, the *plaza de toros,* is standing and chanting at each pass.

Picasso is exultant and shouts himself hoarse.

"*¡Para los pies! ¡Anda, Luis Miguelito!*"

He leans toward Pablito and ruffles his hair.

"*Niño,*" he says laughing, "*parar, templar, mandar* are the three commandments of bullfighting. *Parar* is keeping your two feet motionless, *templar* is moving the material slowly, *mandar* is controlling the bull with the material."

Picasso turns to Cocteau and calls out to him, pointing to my brother.

"You see, Jean, this one will be a *torero!*"

"*Parar, templar, mandar,*" Pablito stammers, starry-eyed.

His grandfather has graced him with his consideration. He must show himself worthy of it.

My father has moved closer to me.

"Is everything okay, Marina?"

I'm happy and I burst out laughing. Everything's okay. I have a family.

A bugle call and the first act begins: *la suerte de varas,* the trial of the lances.

The crowd boos: The picadors are making their entrance,

paunchy and arrogant in their brocade tunics. The horses, weighed down by their riders and by their quilted coverings, limp to their designated place for the fight—a path traced out with lime on the sand.

They are blindfolded.

"It's to calm them," my father explains.

"When one is nothing, one doesn't look death straight in the face," Picasso breaks in. The only death that counts in the arena is the bull's death—homage to the Minotaur who feeds off flesh.

In his shady corner, his *querencia*, his refuge, the bull is digging up the sand with his hooves.

The *peones* rush toward the ring. Whirling their capes, they provoke, assail and goad the bull. Hysterical, the public spurs them on and encourages the beast.

"*¡Anda, toro! ¡Anda!*"

The beast's nostrils are frothing with rage. One *peón*, more daring than the others, ventures into the *querencia*, where the beast has retreated.

Time has stopped.

The bull rises to his feet, his nostrils take in the air and his horns butt against the sky. He charges, swift as lightning, evades the cape held out by the *peón*, rushes straight ahead, then leaps around, back toward the cape, which brushes against his side.

In front of him, the *picador* tries to keep his horse from

rearing. A pause, a reprieve and a new charge. The horse is lifted from the ground and forced against the barrier. Under the impact, he has collapsed on his front legs but still manages to remain standing. In spite of the protective padding that's covering the horse's flank, the bull is looking for a way to gore him. The picador sinks his lance into the bulge of muscle on the bull's neck and puts an instant stop to his violent butting. Blood gushes out, like a geyser. Scarlet and terrifying. Another lance is thrown and the steel nicks the bull's flesh again. He digs in with all fours, is impaled by more and more lances. Again and again. In bullfighting jargon this monstrosity is called the "punishment."

Punishment for what? For having been trapped by man's inhumanity? So they could demonstrate their barbarity? Their will to power? To confer on men a value they don't possess? To be depicted on a canvas one day: *Still Life with Bull's Skull, Guernica, Minotaur, Minotauromachy*?

Another bugle call is heard in the distance. The *picadores* have left the arena.

I feel crushed. I have sustained too many lances.

I'm not interested in the rest of the fight. Nor am I interested in this audience of would-be gladiators—Picasso who is being bombarded by photographers, my father who is drinking uncountable cans of beer, my mother who is surely at this moment laughing somewhere with her hoods, Cocteau the magnificent buffoon, Jacqueline in her black shawl.

I feel the sting of the *banderilleros'* barbs. I wish the film could be run backward, so the bull would recover all his glory; the bloody lances soiling his coat would disappear as well as the barbs planted on his neck. I wish the *barrera* and the steps would vanish into thin air, and that a strong gust of wind would blow away the *toreros* and their idolatrous public. I wish the bull could be back in his field with his herd. I wish this bullfight had never been.

On splayed legs, the bull awaits the final act—the *faena,* or kill. As an insult or sign of arrogance, Domínguin turns his back on him and walks up to the steps. He doffs his head-dress, and brandishes it in Picasso's direction. He offers him death.

The crowd claps and roars, while Pablito squeezes next to me fearfully. I put my arm around his shoulders. I'm afraid too, just as he is.

Two inseparable creatures, like birds who can only live in couples, Pablito and I are bound to each other, hand in hand, forehead against forehead. We refuse to take part in the ig-nominy of men.

We hear *"olé"* and strident whistling. We are paralyzed with anguish as if brimstone were about to descend from the sky.

"Do you think he will suffer?" whispers Pablito.

Cheers, applause and the sound of bugles. Pablito and I raise our heads fearfully. In the arena, the bull's blood has spilled on the ocher ground.

He is dead. Liberated.

A white handkerchief is waved from the presidential stand. At this signal, Domínguín goes up to the dead bull and slices off one of his ears with his dagger. He throws it to my grandfather.

This ear streaming with blood still haunts me at night. I see it placed on the steps where Pablito and I were sitting. An indecently red tuft of sticky hair and yellowish cartilage.

An homage to my grandfather—the great aficionado of human distress.

Chapter Seven

It's been four months since the festival at Arles, and we are without news from our father. Nor have we seen our grandfather, for whom we are insignificant entities. Yet we are Picassos, Picassos like him. Picassos that people point to in the streets.

"See that little boy and little girl? They are Picasso's grand-children."

"The billionaire painter?"

"Who else?"

The grandchildren of the billionaire painter who wander around penniless in the deserted streets of Golfe-Juan.

Summer has ended. The vacationers have left with the first days of autumn. The beach is desolate, the metal gates of the restaurants are drawn, the sun despairingly veiled. It's the beginning of a new school year. Once again our mother has made decisions for us. She has enrolled us in a Protestant school in Cannes.

"It's a highly respected secondary school," she says. She has a reputation to uphold.

The alarm rings. It's six-thirty. Dazed and sleepy, I get up and shake Pablito.

"Hurry up, we're going to miss the bus."

He gets up like a zombie, gropes for his shirt and his pants, slips them on half asleep and joins me in the bathroom. We wash as quietly as possible. Our mother is still asleep.

There's no time for breakfast. Just enough time to comb our hair, put on our shoes and slip Thermoses into our satchels. These contain our midday meals prepared the night before by Madame Danielle—a volunteer who's been sent by the local welfare office to help our mother with the household tasks. Today it is blanquette of veal.

"It's healthy and nourishing," she said to my mother. "I made enough for two days."

Between our textbooks and notebooks we've squeezed two paper plates, a metal tumbler, a knife and a fork. For dessert, an orange. Yesterday it was an apple.

We grab the key to the apartment from the table, gently lock the door and scramble down the stairs. Day is just breaking.

I have bitter memories of those early mornings. The road we had to walk to the *route nationale* where the bus stopped, the garbage trucks picking up refuse and the railroad crossing with its siren announcing the arrival of a freight train were like a Calvary that we had to endure, come rain or frost. We trudged along, carrying our heavy satchels, with the fear of being late in the pit of our stomachs.

I was also afraid of the crush of passengers in the packed bus down to Cannes. We were too small to compete with their jostling, so we huddled up close to each other to minimize the amount of space we occupied. On bad days the trip lasted forty-five minutes and when we arrived in the Cannes station, we still had a twenty-minute walk to the Protestant school on avenue de Grasse.

IT'S CALLED "the school on the hill." The teachers are nice. They like children. They never scold us. Charitable and humane, they sympathize with my mother's situation. They know that our father isn't around to take care of us and that our grandfather makes no effort to make the life of his grandchildren any easier. They don't sit in judgment or label people. As far as they're concerned, we're no different from other children. We're Marina and Pablo. Pablo, not Pablito. At any rate, not Picassos. Following Protestant principles, they want us to be responsible for our actions and learn to be proud of ourselves. There are no chosen ones on this earth. We should aspire to goodness. We shouldn't expect it from others, but we should dispense it. We were never taught these principles by our parents.

Since they are marvelous teachers, we try hard to please them and do well in all subjects. This makes up for the daily grind.

Since we don't have time to go home to Golfe-Juan and the school on the hill has no canteen, Madame Féraud, the headmistress, has agreed to let us eat lunch in our classroom when all the other students have rejoined their families.

Alone in front of our desks, we take out our Thermoses, lay out our paper plates and unfold the napkins containing our knives and forks. We're ill at ease—afraid of soiling our notebooks, staining the floor or messing up our clothes. We nibble carefully, avoiding any awkward gestures, with one eye on our Thermoses and the other on our metal cups precariously balanced on the slanted desktop. Our gestures are like those of bomb disposal experts defusing an explosive device. Sweat trickles down our foreheads.

Usually, we limit ourselves to dessert. In our struggle to avoid awkward gestures, our best allies are apples, bananas and oranges.

Once we've gobbled down our meal, we can go to the courtyard and hang about until the school gates reopen for the other students.

There we feel free—free to let our imaginations wander.

"Last night, I dreamt I was a bird. I flew over a house," Pablito tells me.

"Me too. What was your house like?"

"Very small, with a chimney and a garden full of flowers."

"What kind of flowers?"

"Stocks, irises, peonies. There was a dog."

"Stocks, irises, peonies, a dog? That's funny, Pablito, I had the same dream."

We have the same dreams, we laugh at the same moments, we have the same enthusiasms and the same feelings, we share the same mysteries. We're identical. We can't live without each other. We're Siamese twins. Nothing will separate us.

DURING OUR FIRST TERM at the school on the hill, we're invited to lunch at the Reverend Monod's, to whom the school owes its reputation. "We" means Pablito, me and Mienne, our mother. Mienne has put her hair up and she is wearing a black outfit that makes her look more virtuous. However, her bust is still just as provocative and her conversation just as peculiar. For once her favorite subject isn't Picasso but her Protestant family in Lyons.

"A respectable family of researchers, biologists and scientists," she tells the reverend. "People from the upper middle class who gave me a religious upbringing."

Her pinky is raised and her talk is proper. The reverend and his wife listen to her indulgently until it is time for us to go. God will know how to recognize his own.

I remember the Lotte family that my mother painted in such holy colors for the reverend's benefit. Among them there was Renée, my mother's cousin, and her daughter Christine, a chubby little girl with braids and pleated skirts. They used to come to Golfe-Juan for vacation and stay with my maternal grandmother. In the afternoon they would join us on the beach, where Mienne would greet them overexuberantly.

I was ashamed, ashamed of her playacting, and of our poverty when they invited us to a restaurant or to join them on vacation. We had to turn them down because we wouldn't be able to reciprocate.

They probably thought my mother was stingy. How could we have the name Picasso and be penniless at the same time?

—

"QUICK, Madame! Marina has fainted!"

We are at school. In a daze, I hear Pablito sobbing and Madame Féraud's voice in the background: "Stretch her out! Unfasten the collar of her blouse! Massage her neck!"

These fainting spells—which Madame Féraud calls panic attacks—have been coming over me more and more often. There is a white veil in front of my eyes, a buzzing in my ears and sweat on my forehead. Neither Pablito nor I have wanted to tell our mother about them. We know what she will say. "It's your age," she will tell me. Or "You're too self-absorbed," or "You ate something that doesn't agree with you," or "You're driving me crazy."

Still, she has a doctor give me a checkup and when he tells her that I have the first signs of tuberculosis, she conveys the news to my father. He doesn't believe it. He thinks it is a ruse to extract money from him and his father.

NICE, SUMMER 1959. I have become a patient of Dr. Barraya at the Pasteur Hospital, where I will return several times for stays of three weeks to a month. I weigh only sixty-five pounds and look like a skeleton. I'm lying on the bed, staring at the intravenous solutions dripping slowly into my arm. I must be careful not to move. If the needle slips out of the vein, the nurse is going to have to puncture it again. My arms are covered with bruises.

One drop, two drops, three drops—eighty-seven drops to go and I'll be able to get up and get dressed. Then it's time for the treatment—two hours of staring up at the ceiling. After that, it will be lunchtime. Time seems to stand still.

Pablito isn't allowed to visit, but one of his drawings is tacked on the wall above my bed: a woman selling vegetables at market in Nice. He liked to draw the colorful stalls, the vendors and shoppers, reproducing them from memory in his room at night. But it's the last drawing he'll make. There won't be any others. My mother has so harped on the fact that he has his grandfather's talent that she has turned him off. He has put his crayons away.

One day, my mother comes to see me. One of her boyfriends has driven her over. She announces that she won't be able to stay for long. She tells me that she's managed to rent out the apartment on the rue Chabrier. She's found a garden apartment in a villa—the Villa Habana—in Golfe-Juan.

"It's like Picasso's place," she says. "You can see the sea from the windows."

"Can I have a dog?"

"Dogs are expensive. We can't afford it."

"What about a cat?"

"We'll see."

Down below, in the parking lot, someone is honking his horn. She raises her head and says: "They're waiting for me. I have to go. Be good."

Not a word from my father. Not once has he come to see me.

It's my ninth birthday.

Shocked that my case is just like that of a child on welfare, Dr. Barraya has decided to write my grandfather to tell him that my condition is serious and that I must be sent to the mountains to convalesce. He has already taken the initiative of enrolling me in a children's center at Villard-de-Lans in the Isère region.

The letter is dry and blunt; it doesn't mince words.

The reply is not immediate. Picasso has other things on his mind.

I complain. I don't want to leave Pablito. I need him and he needs me. If they send me away, I won't let myself be treated; I'll run away, they won't find me.

Dr. Barraya tries to calm me. I refuse to listen. If I'm separated from my brother, I'll let myself die.

What exactly happened? Did Dr. Barraya send my grandfather a second letter? Did my father make an appeal to Picasso? I tend toward another hypothesis: Ashamed of being implicated in a way that might cast a shadow on his name, my grandfather decided to get double credit and suggested that Pablito go with me to Villard-de-Lans.

The ideal grandfather, who pampers his grandchildren—but only for the sake of appearances.

VILLARD-DE-LANS has green pastures, pure air, good milk, bread and butter—and my lungs are healed. Alone with Pablito, who follows me around like a shadow, I feel freer than I've ever been. After all those years in prison with a mother, a father and a grandfather—all self-centered—I need to crawl out of my shell. My victims are the couple that directs the children's center. I tell them everything.

"My grandfather wanted to send us to the Soviet Union. My mother started a suit against him. My father is afraid of him."

I'm a gossip. Nothing can stop me. It's like amateur therapy. I pour my heart out to them and tell them all about the fears I've had.

Appalled, the directress phones my mother to warn her.

"She should be told not to blab," she says. "It could harm Picasso's reputation."

My mother takes over where I left off. On the subject of Picasso, she's inexhaustible.

"His grandchildren are sacred to him. He wanted to adopt them, but I wouldn't let him."

In other words, he's a marvelous grandfather.

—

AFTER MY QUIET PERIOD of convalescence, we return to Golfe-Juan, but not to the apartment on the rue Chabrier. My mother has moved to the Villa Habana. The other great change is that, in our absence, she has found a new boyfriend. His name is Jean. He's a twenty-two-year-old who makes pottery and plastic jewelry—an "artist," in other words. My mother works with him. She describes their future together in glowing terms. Thanks to her name they'll be a smashing

success. Picasso is more talked about than ever. Far from dis-
couraging her, Jean keeps the myth alive. How can they take
advantage of the Picasso label to set up their business?
They've found a shed not far from the house. They take poly-
ester, grind it down, trim it and fit into it dried seahorses
bought at a retailer's. They make pendants, good-luck charms,
large panels representing the seabed. The venture does well.
My mother is happy that she's earning enough and doesn't
have to badger my father, who, of course, always forgets to
send us our money by mail. I help out during the summer vacation and earn a bit myself making necklaces with beads
and eucalyptus calyces. It allows me to contribute my share to
the household expenses and above all feed the two emaciated
cats that I've adopted.

Pablito doesn't want me to give them names. All he says is:
"Spare them the grief."

SHORTLY AFTER OUR RETURN, my father arranges to
meet us at La Frégate, a bar in Golfe-Juan. He has recently married Christine Pauplin, whom we know well because we spent
a vacation with her and my father at the Château de Boisgeloup
in the Eure region, near Gisors. Picasso bought the property
when he was still happily married to my grandmother Olga.

I have only vague recollections of Christine. All I remember is that she was careful not to come between our father and

us. She was relaxed, probably out of indifference, and she let my brother and me play with the children in the neighboring farms—country bumpkins who taught us how to chase birds out of copses and with whom we played hide-and-seek in barns and in the ruins of the little ivy-covered chapel on the Boisgeloup estate. We used to collect eggs in the hen house, milk the cows and drink their frothy milk. I liked the pleasant odor of the stables and the newly cut hay. My hands roamed everywhere, including the mud and the straw, and I stroked the backs of heifers and calves. I felt like nothing could make me dirty. It was a serene life and my father was cheerful. He laughed and was amused to see us autonomous and to be autonomous himself. Grandfather wasn't around to set traps for him.

I don't believe Christine ever idealized my father. She accepted him as he was, with his qualities and faults. I also don't think she ever tried to seduce Picasso. She was probably sorry that my father was a slave to him, but she knew she couldn't change anything. She belonged to that category of women who, when they love a man, accept everything about him.

PABLITO AND I arrive at La Frégate. My father is already there. He's smoking a cigarette. In front of him, there's an ashtray full of butts of Gitanes. He clicks his fingers to call the waiter and orders.

"One hot chocolate and one Coke!"

The chocolate is for me, the Coke for Pablito.

"Everything okay at school? You look well."

Conventional banter: school, our health, our plans for the week.

We have no plans.

Silence. And then he says: "I haven't had time to see you. I've just returned from Paris. Your grandfather needed brushes and other supplies. He knows he can count on me."

We'd like to talk to him about Bernard, the baby he's had with his new wife. A legitimate child, of Picasso stock, like Pablito and me.

We don't dare broach the subject, nor does he.

He's already stood up to pay the bill. A hundred-franc bill taken from a wad of bills in his pocket. He looks surprised. Pablito hasn't touched his Coke.

"You're not going to leave it, are you?" he says reproachfully.

Pablito raises his glass and drinks it in one go—then heads for the toilet door. When he returns his eyes are red from crying. He has thrown up—not because of the Coke, but because of a father who doesn't know how to love.

⟶

THE PROTESTANT SCHOOL was more concerned with providing its students with a good education than with getting them to pay. As a result, the Reverend Monod has warned my mother, the school would have to close due to lack of funds. We're in despair. What will become of us?

Our mother takes action immediately. In spite of her quarrels with my grandfather, she writes to him explaining that she had managed to place us in a school on her own, but that now she needs his help. He must contribute to our education. She goes to great lengths to make her case to him. She sends another letter to Maître Antébi, my grandfather's attorney, and asks the director of the Cours Chateaubriand to step in. He writes to Picasso as well, saying he's kept a space for us in his school and is waiting for an answer. It finally arrives: "See my attorney."

"Two erasers, two rulers, two compasses, two books, two notebooks . . ."

Pablito and I choose our school supplies in the small bookstore where arrangements have been made with our grandfather through Maître Antébi. Two erasers, two rulers, two compasses, two books, two notebooks. We're not allowed to take anything not on the list that's been given to him. Everything is added up to the cent. If we need an additional book, we must consult the confounded attorney who manages my grandfather's money. His duty is to be vigilant.

The Cours Chateaubriand is a posh establishment; among the students are many children from well-to-do families who have been placed there so their parents can freely cope with divorce, adultery, stock market or money problems. Children who are doomed to perpetuate a reputation, a name and a fortune. Neglected rich kids who, while they wait for their turn in the limelight, spend their weekends and often their vacations walled up inside the Cours Chateaubriand.

Just like us, they are masters in the art of hiding their family backgrounds. Just like us, they're ashamed of being orphans with famous names. Pablito and I avoid becoming too friendly with them. Only the teachers summon us back to reality. The fame that we are supposed to represent is an honor to them. Later, they'll proclaim everywhere, "I taught history, math or French to the little Picasso kids." A prestigious distinction for educational service comparable to the *palmes académiques*.

No more Thermoses and veal stew, no more lunches eaten in the classroom like paupers. The Cours Chateaubriand has a real restaurant, not a canteen, with white tablecloths and a feast of good things. Such abundance spoils our appetites.

Be that as it may, the little Picasso kids can't afford the gym outfits their instructor has asked them to buy. The director must wait for Maître Antébi to give his consent and he must first discuss the matter with their grandfather.

On another occasion, the little Picasso kids are summoned into the director's office. He informs them that their grandfather still hasn't paid for the past two trimesters, even though they've sent him several letters to remind him that the tuition is past due. Unpleasant as it is, the little Picasso kids will have to talk to their mother about this.

"This matter doesn't concern me," she writes back to the director. "I refer you to Picasso and his administrative staff."

Two months later, the room and board is paid for the full year. Room and board, but not the books that we've had to buy since then. We must start all over again, with new requests. The little Picasso kids are fed up with being scapegoats.

⟶

ANOTHER SPRING at Cours Chateaubriand. Pablito and I are now teenagers. After lunch, the students go to the terrace of a brasserie near the school for coffee. We can't go with them. They're wealthy and we're poor. Since there are no classes this afternoon, they'll probably be going to the movies or the beach at Cannes. Beach mats and umbrellas, pedal boats, soft drinks. They can afford everything with their pocket money.

Pocket money: a term that's not in our personal vocabulary.

Sometimes we get invited to their houses for surprise parties, or on their fathers' boats.

We have to lie, make up a story to turn down the invitations we can't return: "We can't just go out like that," we say.

How can we explain that our mother can't make ends meet, that our father has forgotten to send the infamous allowance, that we're the furthest thing from the mind of the richest painter in the world?

It's true. We're very protected.

—

BOULEVARD CARNOT, the station, the overheated bus and, at the end of the road, Golfe-Juan: This was our banal daily life. Occasionally, we would go to the beach with our local pals. They didn't ask any questions. They knew everything about us. They couldn't have cared less about Picasso. They were our family.

Freedom and escape were intertwined in my mind. I had dreams of traveling around the world. The names of some cities were particularly evocative—Singapore, Melbourne, Baghdad, Calcutta. I craved faraway, wide-open spaces.

To indulge this dream, I used to borrow a moped from one of our friends and go off alone down the little coastal roads, with the wind blowing through my hair—Antibes, Cap d'Antibes, La Napoule, Théoule. I didn't give a thought to time or the danger I was exposed to. The only thing that mattered was the distance separating me from my youthful past. I would stop for a dip in the rocky, red inlets of the Esterel. After the swim, I would bite into a tomato and a piece of bread that I'd brought with me. I was living an itinerant, adventurous life. I was a nomad.

Once the police stopped me on the road into Saint-

Tropez. I had no identification papers on me and refused to tell them my name. They let me go because I was nice and I looked happy.

When I didn't have a moped, my friends and I used to hitchhike.

"We've missed the bus. Could you drop us off at Juan-les-Pins?"

It always worked. The angelic smile, the innocent look, and we would embark for the enchanted isle of Cythera in unfamiliar cars.

The Cours Chateaubriand closes its doors for the summer vacation. This is the year before the baccalaureate exams. I'm sixteen years old. The students stand in front of the school entrance talking about their plans.

"Where are you going this year? To the West Indies?"

"No, I'm going to join my mother in Miami. After that, I don't know, I'll probably go to my father's in Ireland. He just remarried."

Now they turn to us.

"Of course, you're going to Spain with your grandfather?"

"Yes, of course."

"Yes of course."

Once again, we're playing the game of being the lucky kids Picasso dotes on.

Chapter Eight

In 1961, Grandfather bought a Provençal farmhouse in Mougins: Notre-Dame-de-Vie. He needed to get away from La Californie, which had been desecrated by real estate developers who had built a block of residential flats at the edge of its grounds, obstructing the view of the sea and of the Îles de Lérins.

Notre-Dame-de-Vie was a veritable bunker protected by electrified railings and barbed wire. Visitors were screened at the entrance by an intercom system, and Afghan hounds, trained to attack, roamed the grounds day and night. Our visits were transformed into official interviews carefully timed by the implacable Jacqueline, guardian of the sanctuary.

Was Picasso aware of the wall she had erected? I'm afraid he was. He alone had the authority to confer this power on her while remaining in the background.

Both hurt and bitter about Françoise Gilot's book *Life with Picasso* after it was published in 1964, he no longer saw Claude and Paloma, nor, for petty reasons, Maya, his daughter with Marie-Thérèse Walter. Only my father was still admitted, and he wanted Pablito and me to come with him to show that he took care of us. Why didn't he ever allow us to see our grandfather without him, not even once? We might have shown him that we were not just appendages. We might have opened our hearts to him, shared our childhood secrets with him, and he might have understood what we expected of him.

Alas, the iron curtain that had been lowered between Grandfather and us was much too heavy—and forever closed against our questions, our desires, our suffering. What had become of the light of La Californie? At Notre-Dame-de-Vie everything was gloomy—the funereal cypress trees, the lugubrious olive trees, the impregnable enclosure and the metallic voice emanating from the cyclops eye of the intercom.

⁓

A VISIT to Notre-Dame-de-Vie in the late sixties. Our father has picked us up at the crossroads between Cannes and Vallauris.

"Get in quick," he says through the rolled-down window of

his car. "We're late." Late for the divine audience that Grandfather is graciously granting his son and grandchildren.

The gate to Notre-Dame-de-Vie is hermetically sealed. My father rings the bell—two short rings, one long one. We hear Jacqueline's voice on the intercom.

"Who is it?"

She knows it's our father and that he's with us. He's the only person to ring the bell this way to signal his arrival. She wants to let us know, even before we enter, that we're undesirables. She wants to humiliate us. Monseigneur is hers and hers alone. No one has the right to trespass and destroy the web she's spun around her lord and master. She distils her venom. She is the black widow.

"Who is it?"

She doesn't give up. She wants an answer.

"It's Paulo."

The electric lock clicks open aggressively. Brutally, like a reproach. Immediately, the Afghan hounds growl at us, baring their teeth. They are the fierce watchdogs of the realm of darkness that we are entering and they follow us around diligently. They would like nothing better than to jump on us.

Unhurriedly, we walk up the gravel path edged with cypress trees and boxwood. Jacqueline is waiting for us at the threshold of the house, with its cold and austere walls. She is wearing black. Her waist has filled out and her face is drawn.

"Monseigneur is in the small drawing room," she says to my father. "He was going to take a nap."

In other words: "Don't linger."

Grandfather greets us, sitting in an armchair. On the table in front of him is a steaming cup and a flask containing drops that Jacqueline has asked him to take. Our father told us in the car driving over that, for some time now, his father has been very worried about his health. In fact, no one is fooled. Everyone knows that he isn't sick and never has been. His physician—who was also Matisse's—only comes for form's sake. He knows that his patient's ailments are due to his fear of aging.

One thing reassures Picasso, however. All his friends have died but he's still around. All of them—Cocteau, Matisse, Braque, André Breton, André Derain, Paul Éluard, his communist comrade, and Jaime Sabartès, his faithful companion at Els Quatre Gats, the Barcelona café that, in 1900, hosted the first one-man show of a young painter by the name of Pablo Ruiz y Picasso. As well as all the others who were his intimate friends and whom he rejected because he stopped liking them—a distressing slaughter, arbitrary "kills."

Grandfather is immortal. Pablito and I know this. He is the strongest man in the world. He has all the power. He can't die.

We walk up to him shyly in the large vaulted room where he receives the few people who are still admitted to Notre-Dame-de-Vie. He stares at us with his phosphorous gaze from behind the corrective glasses he has only recently started wearing. He hardly smiles at us.

"So how's school?" he asks Pablito.

And then he adds as an afterthought: "And how's your mother, Marina?"

We just nod. What answers can we give to such questions?

"Are you going away on vacation?" he asks without even looking at us.

"No," Pablito replies in a choking voice.

"That's good. . . . That's good," he answers evasively.

What does he care about our vacation? Or our studies? He isn't interested in anything outside of himself.

Jacqueline comes into the room like a shadow. She walks up to my father and whispers in his ear. My father nods with a pained look and turns toward us.

"Marina, Pablito," he says in a pathetic voice, "it's time to go. Pablo needs to be alone. You've made him tired."

We've made him tired though he hasn't bestowed one second of attention on us, one drop of esteem or one ounce of interest.

The holy service is over. Resigned, we follow Jacqueline docilely to the door of the sanctuary where grandfather has blessed us with his indifference.

Jacqueline leaves us at the entrance steps. She shakes hands with us grudgingly and goes right back to join the Sun.

"I'm coming! I'm coming!" she squeals as she rushes into the shuttered house. "I'm coming, Monseigneur!"

She can't bear the idea of abandoning her executioner for even a second. Without him, she can't breathe, she is like a fish out of water.

I will have nothing to do with this wretchedness. I've had enough of the violence of some, the weakness of others, the control of a despot over my life and Pablito's. I want my freedom, my own breathing space. I want to be extricated from this family.

"Pablito, we must work."

"What for? You know we'll never break away. We're Picassos."

In short, we're doomed to suffer.

I've decided that I won't suffer anymore. I want to be autonomous and to defy my destiny.

My grandfather never stopped to think about the fate of those close to him. The only thing he cared about was his painting, and the suffering or happiness that painting provided. As soon as he mastered it, he accepted any formula that allowed him to serve it or disobey it. Just as he crushed tubes of paint to extract the emotion of color, he didn't hesitate to crush those who pined for a glance from him. He loved children for the pastel of their innocence, and women for the sexual, carnivorous impulses they aroused in him. Mixing blood and sperm, he exalted women in his paintings, imposed his violence on them, and sentenced them to death once he felt their mystery had been discharged and the sexual power they instilled in him had dulled. The voluptuousness he derived from sex and from painting was of the same essence. Through both, he tried to resolve his passion and contempt for women. He saw them as harbingers of death. As the monarch of the realm of darkness, he worked on them at night in his studio. They had to be present, subservient and obedient. He worked them with his paintbrush to the point of exhaustion: *verónicas* in blue and orange; *faenas,* kills, in fiery reds, crimsons and blacks, the colors of conflagration. Women were his prey. He was the Minotaur. These were bloody, indecent bullfights from which he always emerged the dazzling victor.

Anything outside this malevolent alchemy did not interest him. All those who escaped or were no longer an object of his gluttony left him cold. They lay in a cemetery of oblivion, with no cross or recognition, no gratitude or compassion. Whether they were women, friends, children or grandchildren, his victims had to be sacrificed to his art.

He was Picasso. He was a genius.

A genius shows no mercy. His glory depends on it.

Chapter Nine

In the summer on the Côte d'Azur, there are many outdoor day camps for the children of working parents. I note the addresses of several of these camps and send my résumé. "Baccalaureate level, serious and conscientious, seeking job as a counselor." I receive answers and must present myself.

"Your name?"

"Marina Ruiz Picasso."

"The daughter?"

"No, the granddaughter."

"Oh, the granddaughter!"

How do I look to these people? Like a problem child who wants to work just to stand up to her family? A rich kid who wants to take food away from the poor?

Looking for work when your name is Picasso? What nerve! What a disgrace! What contempt for others!

What can I do but tell the truth? I stutter, of course: "I love children and, later if I study medicine, I'd like to specialize in pediatrics. If you take me and trust me, I'll make myself as useful as I can."

Always beating around the bush, trying to erase the Picasso stamp, always having to turn the other cheek when confronted with sarcastic remarks, accepting any lousy job and, above all, going to great lengths to be liked. Not by the people in charge who have accepted me on a trial basis but by the children. I win them over, and they begin to tell me their dreams: "Later, I'll take Mommy on a trip around the world. We'll never leave each other."

"Later, I'll drive a locomotive. I'll be a railroad worker like my dad."

These "laters" are full of hope. They make my heart bleed.

I don't have a "later."

⟜

THIS SUMMER I am sixteen, and things are different. Instead of working in a holiday camp, I've got a temporary job in the Golfe-Juan post office. I deliver telegrams to the city residents and vacationers—a job that fills me with tremendous pride.

"Do you have a way of getting around?" asked the postmaster when I introduce myself.

"Of course I do!"

I'm lying, but I have no choice. I must get this job, particularly since the postmaster has also agreed to hire Pablito to sort the mail, for summer is the season when the mail arrives in overflowing sacks. I run over to the cycle shop and explain my problem to the owner. He agrees to sell me a moped on credit, with the first payment at the end of June and the final payment in early October. And at no extra cost, he agrees to check the brakes, replace the cylinders in the engine and straighten out the front mudguard. It's a deal! I can finally call myself a telegram delivery girl, and Pablito a postal sorting clerk and co-owner of a used moped.

With a mailbag slung over my shoulder, I go up and down the streets, ringing bells at garden gates and buzzing the intercoms at apartment buildings.

"Telegram for you!"

In fair weather, there are very few telegrams that bring bad tidings. Usually they announce the arrival of a relative, the birth of a child, some happy event—and they fetch me a tip that will allow me to get new tires for Pegasus, our moped.

Pablito is happy as well. Of all the post office employees, he's the fastest at sorting letters and separating newspapers from the mail. He feels competent. His cheeks are rosy.

Every week, we give our entire salary to our mother. We consider this normal. We must stick together.

I don't recall ever buying clothes without telling her. My couturier and Pablito's is the five-and-dime. A skirt from its racks, a cotton blouse, a T-shirt, canvas pants—this was all we needed for the whole season. We took good care of these clothes. They had to last until the beginning of school.

—

SUNDAY WAS ALWAYS a gloomy day. The beach would be packed with bathers and it made us nauseated. The café terraces and their hoards of tourists depressed us. We had neither the means nor the desire to mingle with this crowd, so we used to go home and stay in our room until Monday morning. Since our father made no effort to see us, we were cut off from our grandfather.

Picasso would be celebrating his eighty-sixth birthday in October. One day, Pablito decided to telephone him. Jacqueline answered.

"Who are you?"

"His grandson."

"Who?"

"I'd like to speak to my grandfather."

"But who are you?"

"Pablo."

"Pablo? There's only one Pablo, young man. And that Pablo can't see you."

She might just as well have plunged a knife into my brother's heart. It was a sacrilege for him to bear the name he'd been given. A usurper, that's what he was, a rascal, someone with no rank, beneath contempt.

And Jacqueline added, in her sour, disdainful voice: "The master isn't home, but you can write to him."

How many tears did I shed during my analysis, recalling the letters that Pablito and I wrote to our grandfather, who never bothered to answer them? Letters that Jacqueline may have torn up. Letters that Grandfather in any case didn't read. Letters that were like messages in bottles thrown into the sea.

Letters in which we tried to tell him that we were capable of loving, helping and understanding him. Letters that said, essentially:

"We're your grandchildren and we need you. We don't want to be little visiting monkeys hiding behind a father for whom you have contempt. We want to see you alone and find out what is on your mind. We want you to tell us about your childhood in Málaga, about José Ruiz, your father, and Doña Maria Picasso y López, your mother, whose name you took and whose height and eyes you inherited. What about your little sister Lola? And your uncle Salvador who, when you were born, blew smoke from his cigar in your nose to revive you when the midwife thought you were dead? And Maria de los Remedios, your godmother, who breast-fed you because your mother, Doña Maria, was too exhausted to give you her breast? You see, since you stole our father, we must appeal to you for a genealogical tree, or a backbone. To construct the present, we need a past. Give it to us, Grandfather. For once, please, give it to us!"

—

October. School starts again at the Cours Chateaubriand. It is the last year of high school for Pablito and me. We have always been inseparable, and now we will graduate together. Pablito had gone to great lengths in elementary school to repeat a grade, failing deliberately so he could be in my class the following year. After that, we never parted.

We're studying philosophy, reappraising things thanks to Gide, Nietzsche, Proust, Rimbaud, Stendhal. We vie with other students over what we know and how we feel; we tear one another apart for a thought, an idea or an ideology. We investigate the human soul, go into ecstasies over an aphorism ("The voyager is still what matters most in a voyage"), argue, quibble, burn, swoon. With theses and antitheses, we assert our personalities.

In the course of these verbal sparring matches, boys and girls are attracted to each other and try to seduce each other. Thanks to the magic of words, a glance or a smile, couples are formed, in response to a sentence by Camus, or a line by Prévert.

And don't be mad if I say tu *to you.*
I say tu *to everyone I like,*
Even if I've seen them only once.

I liked these discreet, self-conscious courtships. I was attracted to the attentive, gallant, romantic boys, who self-effacingly opened doors for me, controlled their ardor, and behaved courteously. Fingers touching lightly, or a kiss on the cheek, were enough to set my heart pounding. It was the only gift they received from me. The only things I demanded was that they respect me, that Pablito like them and that they like Pablito.

I was starry-eyed and, when one of them gave me a cheap ring he had won at a fair, I began to daydream wildly. I was so attached to symbolic gestures that the ring fired up my imagination. I would finally be able to erase the hot-iron brand of Picasso.

I was gullible then.

PABLITO HAS a crush on a girl in our class. Her name is Dominique and she's Corsican. She's pretty, gentle, sane, reflective and deep. She has every desirable quality.

Pablito would like to tell her of his love, but how do you say "I love you" when there's never been love in your childhood?

Discreet and secretive, Pablito doesn't dare speak to his young Corsican. "She'll hear my glances," he hopes.

Dominique doesn't hear Pablito's glances. How could she know that Pablito is attracted to her if he doesn't speak up?

"What should I do?" he asks me one evening in our room.

"Do you want me to talk to her?"

"I have so many things to tell her."

"You should write her."

Words are unruly things. Pablito keeps putting off his letter; he seems unable to express his feelings. He is too anguished, too wounded; too many of his hopes have been smashed.

It's all too much, and Pablito has put it off for too long. Dominique has found someone else.

Love can't wait.

—

MY FATHER phones the Cours Chateaubriand. He wants to see us, but Pablito refuses. He doesn't want to suffer anymore.

My father has arranged to meet me at the terrace of a café across the street from the train station in Cannes. He's with a young woman whom he's brought back from Paris. A young woman? Céline—that's her name—must be nineteen. She's two years older than I am. He whispers into my ear: "Céline is just a friend. Nothing more than a friend."

From my amused look, he understands that I don't believe a word of it. Whether Céline is a friend or girlfriend, he doesn't have to worry. I certainly won't mention her to my mother or to Christine, if I happen to run into her. His playboy aura has long ceased to appall me. In a way, he's a stranger to me.

"Your brother didn't want to come?" he asks me in a pitiful voice.

"He couldn't."

No more words are exchanged. My father and I have so few things to say to each other—and we are so inhibited.

Fortunately, Céline is here, with her affected mannerisms, her giggles, her fluttering eyelashes. She's proud of being with the son and granddaughter of Picasso, the super famous painter. She feels like a celebrity.

❧

We have moved from the Villa Habana to the Villa La Rémajo, a house my mother has found in the hills above Golfe-Juan. Having sold the apartment in town, my mother can afford a nicer place. It has a garden full of flowers, and a view of pink sunsets over the sea and the Esterel mountains.

We're only a few months away from the baccalaureate exams. Pablito is sitting cross-legged on his bed. His lips quiver as he mumbles a few lines of Baudelaire's "La Destruction" in a low voice:

Constantly the Demon tosses and turns by my side;
He swims around me like an unfathomable melody;
I swallow him and feel him burning my lung . . .

Baudelaire, Rimbaud, Chénier, Verlaine, Apollinaire—insatiably, Pablito consumes the words of the accursed poems that glorify suffering, despair and death. His studies no longer interest him.

"What for?" he keeps repeating. "I have no future."

I lose my temper, reprimand him and try to reason with him: "Come on, pull yourself together. Everyone has a place on earth!"

He shrugs. I annoy him. He becomes aggressive: "Stop lecturing me, and leave me alone. Why look the other way? We're caught in a trap from which we'll never escape."

His eyes are blazing. He gets up, shouting at me as he walks out of the room. "I leave you to your illusions! They might cost you a lot."

It's true, they have cost me a lot.

PABLITO HAS LEFT a note on the living room table: "I won't be back tonight."

My mother is extremely upset.

"Did he tell you where he was going? Why is he doing this to me?"

I don't say a word. I'm determined not to feed her fears. I'm too aware of what her neurosis will lead to—cries, moans, shortness of breath, blackouts, emergency calls to a physician. High drama. A drama I reject.

"Pablito will be back. He must have gone to see a friend."

"After everything I've done for him!"

A narcissistic outburst. Persecution mania. And, above all, depicting herself as the victim.

"Calm down. Pablito will be back."

No sign of Pablito at the Cours Chateaubriand. No one has seen him. Where is he? No one knows and I'm worried. He's been gone now for three days. No news. I make endless rounds of the roads around Golfe-Juan, Vallauris and Valbonne on my moped. I shout his name into the scrubland, the groves, the ravines.

The only answer I get is an echo.

THE FOLLOWING DAY, Pablito still hasn't shown up. The director of the Cours Chateaubriand sends a letter to Maître Antébi, the only relay between my father and us. My father, who has been notified by Maître Antébi, summons me.

"Your brother has been cutting classes for three days. If you see him, tell him I don't want any trouble. Your grandfather has sacrificed enough for him. His schooling is expensive. He could at least show some gratitude."

My father doesn't think of asking why Pablito acts this way. For him, it's childishness, childishness that might tarnish his relationship with his own father. And earn him the inevitable criticism: "You're a good-for-nothing!"

Pablito comes back, as he always does when he runs away, except that now he's running away more and more often. Where does he go? I have no idea. He refuses to tell me. I respect his silence. It's so eloquent that I prefer to remain silent too.

Much later—alas, much too late—my analysis helped me understand that he had lost all hope. Unable to put his suffering into words, he needed another form of escape. He had to walk uninterruptedly in the open spaces, sleep in the hollow of a rock, and go off again, taking roads at random; it helped him shake off the burden of reality. He sought the void. He had a desperate desire for an indefinable elsewhere.

He would come back without saying a word, worn out, his cheeks drawn. From a twig stuck to his sweater you could tell that he had lain down in a field; from sand in his shoes, that he had walked and maybe slept on the beach. Had he thought of eating? Out of respect, I didn't question him.

He was in his own world.

Chapter Ten

In June we take the baccalaureate exam, then await the results. Pablito and I have passed. What a relief! Given the chaos in our life, passing the test is unexpected.

Our fellow students are standing around in front of the gates of the Cours Chateaubriand, talking about their future plans. One of them says, "My parents advised me to go to business school. Later, I'll be taking over the family business."

"I've decided to go to law school," says another. "Afterward I'll be working in my father's law firm."

I know what I want to do. I want to go to medical school and become a pediatrician.

Maître Antébi, whom my mother advised me to see, raises his arms in the air. "Medical school! That's seven years of study! Did you think about the cost? Your grandfather will never agree."

It's true, let's not daydream. Not only will Picasso refuse to help me; I can already guess what he'll say: "Did I study anything? You'd be better off as a waitress in a bar."

A waitress in a bar. True, I could go to medical school and pay for my studies by working at night as a dishwasher in a bar. Many people have done that.

The only difference between those people and Pablito and me is that we have not been raised in a loving household. It's one thing to be a dishwasher or a maid when you know that, after work, you'll go back to a loving mother who provides a home, equilibrium and strength. But how can anyone aspire to a place in the sun when they've always lived in a shadow of unhappiness?

Pablito has also understood that nothing will come his way. A fatalist, he accepts defeat. Can it be called defeat when you don't fight anymore? When you have no desire to fight anymore?

Yet for a long time he had dreams of writing. Writing to try to communicate; writing for the sake of writing. He wanted to leave for Africa and describe the animals; to travel to a glacier and witness the melting of the snows; to isolate himself and record the things that moved and fascinated him.

But you can't make a living that way. To make a living, we must fight and struggle. Not Pablito, who has given up, but me since I'm still alive.

—

THE SUMMER after the exam, with my experience as a camp counselor on my résumé, I find a job in the Vallauris home, in the unit for the seriously handicapped. I take care of a group of autistic, psychotic, schizophrenic and severely retarded children. I get them up, wash and dress them, make them eat, keep them busy, and work with a psychologist who comes twice a week. The children are quite a group. Some chew on their fingers; some howl all day; some remain prostrate, while others walk tirelessly around the room. The most aggressive ones have to be tied down when they go to sleep. They strike me, or throw plates of pasta in my face. I don't scold them; I refuse to tie them to make them eat, as some orderlies do. I wash the hands of the ones who eat their excrement; I have them brush their teeth; I caress their heads.

The smell of excrement clings to my skin and soul for many years—the smell of misery, misfortune and malediction.

The nurse, the maid, the cook and the nurse's aides—they've all learned that I'm Picasso's granddaughter.

"She's sneering at us. What's she doing here?"

The most malicious give me the most demeaning tasks. The union activists want me to support their program.

"With your name, we'll have more clout."

Thanks to analysis, the paths I've chosen cease to be impenetrable.

I didn't choose this kind of work by chance. I worked in the Vallauris home so I would feel less lonely. Unconsciously, I needed to empathize with the misfortune of those handicapped children so I could cope with my own misfortune. It brought my own life into perspective.

They didn't stick to me; I stuck to them.

AROUND THE SAME TIME I start work at the Vallauris home, the Communist town council of Vallauris finds a job for Pablito—the least they could do for Comrade Picasso. The position is as the librarian at the Sun and Seawater Center, a trauma unit for car accident victims, amputees needing physical therapy, people partially or completely paralyzed. Pablito seems content with this. Books are his passion.

But before he's even reported to work, he learns that the position he was promised is not free. The head of personnel offers him another job as an orderly—emptying the chamberpots, cleaning the bedpans, sweeping the floor, changing the patients' soiled sheets. Pablito accepts. After all, he's accepted everything for so long, especially the unacceptable.

My mother inspects me from head to foot.

"You could do something about your appearance," she

Olga Khokhlova as a ballerina in Diaghilev's Ballets Russes in 1917, the year she met Picasso. They would marry the following year.

Olga in Picasso's garage studio at Fontainebleau in the summer of 1921, surrounded by pastel sketches of her for the painting *Three Women at a Fountain* (1921).

Paulo Picasso (born February 4, 1921) in Normandy, summer 1925. The photograph calls to mind the painting *Paulo on a Donkey* (1923).

Olga and Picasso with Paulo at Antibes, summer 1923.

Antibes, summer 1923. Paulo and
Picasso on the beach at La Garoupe.

Paulo and Picasso at La Californie in 1957.

This page and opposite: A New Year's greeting-card collage made by Olga in 1951 from photographs of Picasso, herself, Paulo, Émilienne, Marina, Pablito and other family members.

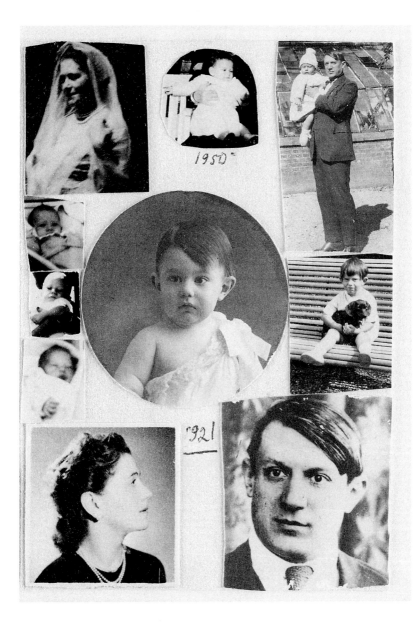

1950

1921

Picasso with Marina (born November 14, 1950), circa 1951.

Paulo holding Pablito (born May 5, 1949) and Marina, circa 1952.

A party at La Galloise in Vallauris, 1956. Pablito and Marina are in the foreground, behind them Picasso with Jean Cocteau. Picasso went to Rome in 1917 to design the sets for *Parade*, a ballet done in collaboration with Cocteau and Erik Satie. It was there that he met Olga Khokhlova.

Pablito in
Vallauris, 1954.

Paulo with Pablito
and Marina in 1954.

Marina and Pablito circa 1957, on the Boisgeloup estate in Normandy, where they spent a summer with their father and Christine Pauplin.

Marina and Pablito with their father at Boisgeloup, circa 1957.

Émilienne with Pablito and Marina at the harbor at Golfe-Juan, summer 1956.

Marina and Pablito in
Villard-de-Lans, Savoie.

Marina and Pablito at Vauvenargues. Behind them is Picasso's bronze sculpture *Man with a Sheep* (1943).

Pablito as a teenager,
circa 1968.

Pablito in 1970.

The Village of Youth, the children's center founded by Marina in Thu Duc, a northern suburb of Ho Chi Minh City, in 1990. It includes a school, a gymnasium, a swimming pool, a park, and a number of small houses designed to create a family atmosphere.

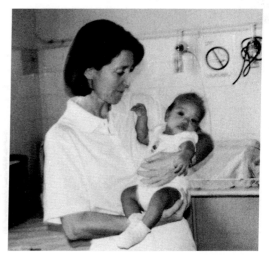

Marina on a visit to one of the children's centers in Vietnam financed by her foundation.

Marina at a day-care center supported by her foundation.

Marina at the Village of Youth in 1992 with her daughter Flore and son Gaël and a child from the center.

Marina and a child from Go Vap, an orphanage that was refurbished by her foundation.

Marina in front of a family house at the Village of Youth, 1992.

Marina at La Californie in 2001, in front of Picasso's *Portrait of Olga* (1923).

says. "You look terrible, you could use makeup. And look at your hair! And your dress. You look like a bum."

Disgusted, she adds, "It's true, you can't wear the same kind of clothes as me. You don't have my bust. Or my legs. Really, life hasn't been kind to you."

I don't answer. I am too tired.

The days go by, each day as the one before. The ring of the alarm clock, tea with no sugar, a shower and the road to work.

In the evening, Pablito is already asleep when I join him in our room. A collection of Rimbaud's poetry is lying on his chest. I open it at a bookmark and read the lines that he has underlined in pencil:

> *Perfumes don't make his nostrils quiver;*
> *He sleeps in the sun, his hand on his chest*
> *Quietly. There are two red holes on his right side . . .*

Pablito is smiling in his sleep.

⌒

MY MOTHER doesn't have a boyfriend anymore and is dependent on the kindness of her few acquaintances to get around, so I buy a little VW. "Economical, solid, never breaks down," says the brochure I find in our mailbox. After much bargaining, the Volkswagen dealer agrees to let me pay it off over five years.

"Only because it's you!"

For once, the Picasso name helps me: I get a credit equal to a quarter of my monthly salary.

My mother is delighted with my acquisition.

"Marina, remember, when you leave work, pick up the groceries I left at the store!"

"Marina, since you've got wheels, stop by the pharmacy and don't forget to get my medical form stamped!"

"Marina, don't forget, you have to drive me to the lab for medical tests!"

I'm her errand boy, her chauffeur, her servant. She doesn't care that I'm dead tired after work; I'm here to serve her.

My father sees me only to talk about Picasso.

"Jacqueline has had an elevator installed for him at Notre-Dame-de-Vie. He's having more and more trouble moving around. He refuses to see me. What do you think of that, Marina?"

He doesn't ask a single question about what I'm up to. All he says is: "I hope your grandfather is well. Call me if you have news."

Pablito is increasingly taciturn. I'm now the only person with whom he is willing to communicate.

"Do you remember the afternoons we used to spend with our grandmother Olga?"

"Yes, of course, Pablito."

"Remember the legends she used to tell us in Russian?"

"She loved us, Pablito."

"I wish I were with her."

SUNDAY, APRIL 8, 1973. As always on Sunday, I'm on duty at the Vallauris home. Apart from a few children who are yelling in their rooms, the ward is relatively quiet. The nurse who is taking over the next shift has just arrived. My day is over. I can leave.

Pablito is in front of the entrance to the building. He has come with his moped. He rushes up to me and cries in a broken voice:

"Grandfather . . . Grandfather. He died."

Grandfather, dead? I can't believe it.

"It's not true, Pablito? How do you know?"

"I heard it on the radio. He died this morning at eleven-forty. A heart attack."

He catches his breath and adds, overcome: "A heart attack following pulmonary edema. That's what they said."

I'm shattered. Grandfather has died without our seeing him again. Died alone with Jacqueline at Notre-Dame-de-Vie. Died in his fortress. In complete solitude.

On television, we see a stampede of journalists, the gate of Notre-Dame-de-Vie topped with its barbed wire, the police vans, and we hear the voice of the announcer: "Yesterday, we were told by his secretary Miguel, Picasso still took his walk around the grounds on the arm of Jacqueline Picasso. She has refused to see us. She is overwhelmed with grief. The family physician is watching over her health."

We must talk to our father. Pablito telephones Paris. A voice answers that our father has left for the Côte d'Azur.

For the Côte d'Azur, but where on the Côte d'Azur?

Pablito phones the hotels where our father usually stays. On the fourth call, the porter tells him that Paulo has just left for Notre-Dame-de-Vie.

"Try reaching him this evening."

We have no luck in the evening. When we try the next day, our father answers and tells Pablito: "The funeral is tomorrow, in the strictest privacy. Jacqueline asked that none of you attend. I'll call you back."

Pablito is indignant, and his nerves are on edge. He is on the verge of tears.

"Even if I must lay siege, I will see my grandfather," he says. "I have the right to. No one can take it away from me."

I try to calm him down.

"Pablito, we haven't been allowed to see him for such a long time. It's useless."

IN SPITE OF MY ADVICE, that very afternoon Pablito jumps on his moped and goes to Notre-Dame-de-Vie. He rings the bell at the gate. No one answers. He keeps ringing. A guard suddenly appears with the two Afghans at his side.

"Go away!" he yells. "You can't come in. I have orders from Madame Picasso."

Pablito is obstinate.

"I order you to open the gate. Tomorrow my grandfather is being buried. I want to say good-bye to him."

"Clear off!" screams the guard. "Get out of sight, or I'll release the dogs!" Like a devil, he runs out of the gate, grabs Pablito's moped and throws it into a ditch.

Behind the fence, the dogs are growling and licking their chops.

Inside Notre-Dame-de-Vie, Picasso is lying in his coffin, wrapped in an embroidered black Spanish cape. Jacqueline and my father are by his side. They haven't heard a thing.

Lying in bed, Pablito refuses to speak or eat or see anyone. I spend the night on the living room couch so he can be alone. For once, my mother behaves discreetly. She's careful not to show it, but I think that my grandfather's death is an enormous weight off her mind. She will no longer suffer and, above all, we will no longer suffer.

"What's the point of getting into such a state?" she whispers to me.

A state for which she is partly responsible and accountable, I think to myself.

Our lifelong friend Alain, who in happier times used to help us fix up the dinghy on the beach in Golfe-Juan, is here. Timidly, he pops his head into Pablito's room.

"Are you okay?"

"Yes," my brother replies.

"Do you want to talk?"

"No, I prefer to rest. I need sleep."

My mother has also gone to bed. Before leaving us, she whispers: "Don't forget, tomorrow you have to pick me up at the hospital after my tests." Endless tests from which she'll come out satisfied and cured—until the next round.

My sleep is full of nightmares, of Grandfather and his eyes. Flashing, inhuman, like those of a bird of prey. Those blazing, hostile, merciless pupils. And that laugh—enormous, sardonic, cruel.

I wake up with a start, dripping with sweat.

In his room, Pablito is fast asleep. He has left the bedside lamp on.

APRIL 12, NINE O'CLOCK. Picasso has been dead for four days. My brother seems calm.

"Did you sleep well, Pablito?"

"Very well," he replies, in a choking voice.

"I'm going to pick up Mienne at the hospital. Do you need anything?"

"Everything's fine, Marina."

I'm driving the car. Mienne is next to me. She senses that

I don't feel like talking. Talk about what? Her blood pressure? Her cholesterol?

La Fontonne, Antibes, Juan-les-Pins, Golfe-Juan, avenue Juliette-Adam, the chemin de la Rampe and, at the very end, the Villa La Rémajo, where Pablito should be waiting for us. I'm driving with the accelerator flat against the floor, cursing the red lights and all the cars that are slowing traffic.

I open the door. The cats slip out between my legs, their fur bristling. They seem eager to get out of the house. I have a sudden premonition and I run into the living room. Pablito is there, lying on the sofa. There's blood on his hair, his face, his chest. I rush over to him. Blood gushes from his mouth. And there's a suffocating, horrible, toxic odor, the unpleasant smell of a hospital or morgue.

"Pablito! Talk to me!"

He groans. He is breathing.

My mother is panic-stricken. Her distress is so great that she can't utter a word or a cry. She's holding a crumpled little plastic bag, which had contained a dose of bleach.

The odor, the hemorrhage, the foam on his lips—Pablito had emptied it.

Fast. We must act fast. I call the emergency services. My God, please make them hurry. I look at my watch. It is eleven-thirty.

I must be strong. I must not fall apart.

Finally they come with a stretcher. They put Pablito into

the red ambulance. I climb up next to him and hold his hand.

"Pablito, it's your little sister!"

A stream of blood comes out of his mouth. All his blood is flowing out of him.

The siren is howling wildly; we bump up and down the sidewalks as the driver meanders around the traffic. Racing against time, racing against death.

We arrive in Antibes, at the emergency unit of La Fontonne Hospital, where I had gone to pick up my mother that morning.

The glass door closes in front of me. I'm separated from Pablito.

"Hang on! Don't give up, Pablito!"

The wait. My head is empty from too much suffering, too much anger, too much fear. Finally, a doctor appears. He comes up to me and says: "We can't tell yet. We must wait until he's gotten beyond the forty-eight-hour mark."

"Hang in there, Pablito!"

Chapter Eleven

The emergency room. Pablito is lying on his bed, inert. He breathes jerkily through tubes in his mouth. His irregular heartbeats are monitored on a screen. A machine checks his blood pressure. An Ariadne's thread separates him from death; a tangle of IVs connects him to life. His hand inside mine is so soft. So soft and fragile.

First Pablito had to be brought back to life and now, after many weeks, he is in the intensive care unit. He has undergone a whole series of operations on his esophagus, his stomach and his intestines, all severely damaged by the chlorine he drank. He is being fed intravenously. The physicians are considering grafts or transplants but with very little conviction. Then they give up on the idea. The lesions are too serious and it is the kind of surgery for which he would have to be transferred to a state-of-the-art unit in Marseilles or Paris. Even if it could save his life, where would we find the money for this transfer? My father or Jacqueline, as heirs of my grandfather, could easily get the money at a bank, but they don't come forward. Picasso's death has locked them into a nebulous, unhealthy world of their own. They have lost their base, lost their master. Pablito's suicide attempt doesn't count for them. They are floundering in their self-centeredness.

Pablito can finally speak. He can finally answer my questions. "Why did you do this?"

"There was no more hope. No other way out."

"Pablito, we're young. We could find a way out if you would trust me."

He has the courage to smile. "Well, you see, I wanted to find a way out. I didn't succeed."

"I'm here, Pablito. You can count on me."

He looks at me and doesn't answer right away. When he finally does speak up, his words are heart-rending: "They didn't want us at his funeral. They didn't want us to be part of their lives. We've never been able to rely on our father, who has never grown up. Now that Grandfather is dead, he's become

Jacqueline's vassal. Cowardliness and baseness. The Picasso empire refused to let you study medicine. The Picasso empire let you take that wretched job; you had to accept it. The Picasso empire closed all doors to you. These things had to stop. So you know what, Marina?" I listen silently. "I ran away for the last time. To save you, I ran away. I had to do it. A gesture that could match theirs."

"Please, Pablito!"

"I wanted to implode, destroy all our suffering from the inside. Now they'll realize that you exist. From now on, they'll take care of you. At least for the sake of public opinion."

Public opinion—that is, the press—pounces on "the suicide of the century." Everything that relates to Picasso stirs up the journalists: "The famous painter's grandson did not want to live after the death of his grandfather. He was twenty-four years old." "In the shadow of Picasso, his grandson Pablito lived in poverty." On the lookout for scandal, the journalists rummage through our private lives, question everyone who has known us, and wallow in gossip. They describe our living conditions in great detail, exploiting and exaggerating things. They turn us into victims and scapegoats: "A few hundred meters from their grandfather's sumptuous villa, they lived in a state of great destitution." My mother may have played a part in that gossip. I don't know and I don't want to know. All I care about is my brother.

There is no sign of life from Maya, Claude, Paloma or my

father. Are they ashamed, or do they fear the revelations of the press? Why don't they put in an appearance? Is despair contagious?

Marie-Thérèse Walter is the only one who has approached us with great kindness and generosity. She came to see my mother and said, "I've got two Picasso paintings. I'll try to sell them." My grandfather's death meant she had no more money since she no longer received the meager allowance that he used to give her. Yet she sold those paintings to help us during Pablito's three-month hospital stay—a gesture of great humanity for which I am immensely grateful. Even though I was able to pay her back later, when I became an heiress, I applaud her goodness and courage. Her sense of playfulness, too, as demonstrated in a letter she sent later: "Now that you're free and ask me what would make me happy in exchange for what I did for you and Pablito, buy me a helicopter." I like to think this helicopter was a witticism. Or a show of modesty. Extreme modesty.

After a month and a half, my father finally shows up at the hospital. A nurse tells me that he's waiting outside the unit. I tell my brother, "Pablito, he'd like to see you." Pablito turns his head toward me. Speaking exhausts him. I lean over him and repeat: "Pablito, he'd like to see you." He smiles sadly and whispers: "Tell him it's too late. I have nothing to say to him."

Pablito now weighs only about sixty pounds. He is fed intravenously. He will never regain his digestive functions. He is condemned to the life of a disabled person. In spite of that, we make plans. "You'll see, we'll never leave each other."

"Will I write?" he asks me.

"Yes, Pablito, you will."

"Tell me what it will be like."

"We'll find a house for the two of us. You'll have your room and I'll have mine. We'll buy curtains for the windows. You'll have a desk, and a typewriter." I depict a sunny future so he will believe in life and forget his suffering.

WEDNESDAY, JULY 11. Pablito has been moved into a room upstairs. The doctors have removed his IVs. I know what this means. There is no more hope. I must not cry; I must try to smile. "You know, Marina, I'm beginning to feel well. I'm no longer in pain." He doesn't know that he's been given morphine. "Rest, Pablito. Soon you'll be well. I have to go now. I'll be back tomorrow." I must leave this room; I want a doctor to speak to me. I want the truth. No matter what it is, I want the truth. From the somber look of the intern on duty, I understand that my brother is doomed. I don't want to believe it. It seems too unjust. "He's not going to die, is he?"

"Go home," he says to me in a soothing voice. "If something happens, I promise to call you."

Curled up in an armchair, I await daybreak. My mother,

drained by sorrow, has gone to bed. I look at my watch. It is a quarter to four. Every second counts. Tomorrow. If only tomorrow would come. Four o'clock. The telephone rings. The blasted telephone. I pick it up, anguished, faltering, frightened. "It's over, your brother has passed away." It is July 12, 1973. After a three-month ordeal, Pablito has breathed his last breath. Medical science wasn't able to do anything for him. Nor could Picasso.

The press goes wild. On the radio, on television, in the magazines, all we hear about is my brother's death. Or rather the death of "Picasso's grandson." "His name was Pablo, like his grandfather." In death, he is finally entitled to his name.

Still no news from my father, although he has obviously learned of his son's death. How could he not know, given the journalists' uproar over the suicide? I no longer care to see my father, but I need him, or rather I need his consent so Pablito can be laid to rest next to his grandmother. Maître Ferreboeuf, a very young attorney in Antibes, agrees to write him. For free, of course—how else? For once, my father replies immediately: "I see no objection." We must still find the money to pay for the funeral. I'm in despair. Where can we find the money? We don't have a penny.

In Cannes the students in the café terraces whisper among themselves. Discreetly, they take bills out of their pockets and hand them to one of their schoolmates. At another table, students add their names to a list. The money they are collecting, without telling me, will pay for Pablito's entire burial. "Pablito, you are resting next to your grandmother Olga. Remember her words: 'Right now, you're the *petit-fils* of the *grand peintre*, but soon you'll be the *grand fils* of the *petit peintre*.'"

Your friends at the Cours Chateaubriand got the message. With their generous impulse, they testified to the fact that you were greater, infinitely greater, than Picasso the painter.

At the Protestant cemetery in Cannes, among our friends and intimates from Cannes and Golfe-Juan, one man is hiding. He is crying. That man is my father. In my grief, I hadn't dared to hope that he would come to ask his son for forgiveness.

Chapter Twelve

I'm indifferent to everything. I get up, take a shower, roam around the house, walk by people and things without seeing them. I'm not even angry or indignant. I have no desire, no expectations. All I know is that Pablito is dead.

Everything else is pointless.

Mienne—in my heart of hearts, I no longer see her as my mother—talks about her distress nonstop. "Your brother. Oh, your poor brother!" She weeps and moans, intoxicating herself on grief. "I'm going to write a book. I'll record it all. Picasso and me, Picasso and your father, Picasso and your brother.

Everything, I'll tell all." The Picasso virus has taken hold of her again. She gives interviews, stops people in the street. The grocer, the baker, the butcher, the hardware store owner and all their customers become her captive audience. "Oh, if only you knew what suffering I'm going through!" She talks about our poverty, the sacrifices she had to make, her self-abnegation, the trials she endured, the insults she had to tolerate, while Picasso, the loathsome Picasso, was rolling in dough. "We had to beg for a morsel of bread." Everyone sympathizes with her sorrow. So much suffering merits compassion.

Her display of grief turns my stomach. I refuse to express my suffering. I say nothing and hide from the world. Locked in silence, I'm regarded as an insensitive person—a heartless creature who is ruthlessly rejected by her mother: "There is no justice. You're the one who should have died." Me, and not Pablito. I'm a girl. I belong to the category of people for whom she has no love. To try to get my mother to love me, I submit to all her demands. I do the housework and make the meals; I do everything she asks. I become sickly, anorexic. I waste away. She doesn't care. As far as she's concerned, I don't count. I go back to my job at the home, back to my autistic and schizophrenic children. But now I can't bear their cries, their madness, their wretchedness. I've become too immersed in Pablito's wretchedness. I must get away and put a distance between my mother and me. I want to find myself, give myself a chance, and forget everything so I can finally be alone with the memory of my brother.

I quit my job and leave for London. There I find a student hostel where I can live for very little money. The hostel takes in young women from all over Europe: girls from Germany, Italy, Spain and, of course, England. To distract myself, I go out at night with my friends; I attend soccer games, explore the city, and take on small jobs to make money, as a baby-sitter, an assistant in a record store, a saleswoman in a cloth-ing store. On the days when I feel blue, I phone my mother. In spite of all the harm she has done me, I need to hear her voice. She either hangs up on me or tells me she doesn't have time to talk: "Your timing is always bad." That's true, my timing is always bad.

↼

I WILL DELIBERATELY skip over a whole part of my life. It might have begun like a fairy tale, with "once upon a time," and ended with "they had loads of children." This "once upon a time" began when I was fifteen. My Prince Charm-ing—because, of course, he had to be a prince—was a physi-cian. He was tall and had blue eyes. In my childish innocence, he had every possible virtue. A physician relieves pain, and I had so much pain. He was the kind of man I thought I would marry one day. Naive as I was, I idealized him and saw my-self leaning my head on his shoulder, a physician's shoulder. The man and his profession were connected in my mind.

He was . . . here I'll leave a blank. A blank that I'll fill in only for Gaël and Flore, the children I had with this man. This blank could be the subject of a whole book. But I'll never write it. However, I'm prepared to disclose its contents to Gaël and Flore should they so desire one day. Though I've trained myself to be silent, I promise to tell them the truth, in great detail. Then they will know the lengths I went to in order to give them the love they deserved, even if the price of that love was torment, pain and fear. Gaël, I'd like you to know that *you* can be loved for *your* life. The recipe is simple. Be yourself and don't cheat. The future is not a utopia. Bearing the name Picasso is hardly an accolade. Prefer the name Gaël. I was told that in Irish it means "brave." Be worthy of that name. Flore, you will always amaze me. On horseback as in life, you jump over all the obstacles—magnificently, brilliantly, and always with simplicity. The simplicity I love and of which I'm so proud. If you want me to leaf through these blank pages one day, you need not pull on the bit as you do with your horses. My mouth will find it so hard to confide all the things I endured when I was your age.

EIGHT MONTHS PASS, and I return from London. I call my mother to tell her I don't want to live with her anymore. The future father of my children has asked me to live with him. I must try my luck. Come what may. I'm only twenty-two years old. At Villa La Rémajo, my mother has left my belongings on her doorstep—not in a suitcase but in a garbage bag. I'm an ungrateful daughter. I deserve nothing better than a gray garbage bag.

THURSDAY, JUNE 5, 1975. On the other end of the phone, I hear a voice that I don't recognize. It's Christine, my father's wife. "Marina, your father has just died. He was very sick." It's impossible for me to believe. It is just too dreadful. Grandfather dead, my brother dead, my father dead; no one is left except my mother and me, and it makes me feel guilty.

I would like to make up for the time and distance that separated me from my father, and revive him through Christine's words. "His last wish was to see Spain again. When he returned his condition worsened. He died last night." And of course, the ritualistic phrase: "He didn't suffer." He died two years after my brother. He was fifty-four years old.

On the analyst's couch, I have asked my father's forgiveness so many times, my father whom I never used to see. I asked him to forgive the harm his father had done him, to forgive my brother, who had banished him from his memory, to forgive me for daring to pass judgment on him. Who gave any thought to his life? No one. He wasn't famous.

Later that day, I get a phone call from Claude, the son of

Picasso and Françoise Gilot. Since 1974 he, his sister Paloma and Marie-Thérèse Walter's daughter, Maya Widmayer, have had a legal right to the name Picasso and are recognized as heirs.

"Marina, do you want to come to your father's funeral?"

"How can I? I don't have any money."

"I'll send you your ticket."

Claude comes to pick me up at Orly airport in Paris. I sense he's self-conscious, and I'm self-conscious. We haven't seen each other in ages. He's surprised that I have no luggage—only the blue jeans and clogs I'm wearing. I'm not trying to make a statement; it's just that since my brother's death I'm not even interested in buying the bare essentials. "Tomorrow," says Claude, "you'll go see Maître Zecri, the lawyer in charge of your grandfather's estate. He will give you a check." A check? Why? I don't understand. "In the meantime," Claude adds, "take this one-hundred-franc bill. You can't go around Paris without any money on you." He takes me to his house, on the boulevard Saint-Germain, a luxurious apartment where his new girlfriend and other people I don't know are waiting for us. "Did you have a good trip? Do you want anything to drink? Do you want to be taken to your room now?" They are so considerate and kind.

It may seem strange, but when Claude asks me if I want to go to the hospital where my father's body is laid out, I say yes without a moment's hesitation. After many years apart, I want

to see him again. Maybe for Pablito's sake and my own—
especially for Pablito, who had been turned away from Notre-
Dame-de-Vie when grandfather died—I want to see him
again. And make him exist.

My father is lying on a white bed. His face is contorted.
Even in death, I have the feeling he's suffering. I get closer and
put my hand on his crossed hands. Maybe I kiss him. Do I
kiss him or simply touch him?

Now I don't know, but in that dimly lit room, I wanted to
make certain that it was really he—he who, alive, had been so
absent and so weak. A cheek . . . a cold hand. That's all that
was left.

The next day, Claude tells me that he is taking me to his
country house for the weekend. "The funeral isn't until
Tuesday. A refreshing break in the country will do you
good."

The weekend in Normandy is a bad memory. First, I don't
know anyone and I feel left out. Second, being short of space,
Claude puts me up in an isolated annex by myself, where I
spend the night trembling with fear.

On Sunday night we return to Paris. We have a dismal
dinner at the Brasserie Lipp, in Saint-Germain-des-Prés; I
can't follow the conversation. Then we go back to Claude's
apartment. "Good night, Marina. We wish Pablito had been
with us tonight." It's the first time my brother is mentioned.
His suicide is disturbing. His death is indecent.

FOR THE SPANISH, funerals are a party, an opportunity
to see relatives, cousins and friends one hasn't seen in a long
time. An *oportunidad,* as they say over there. There's a dinner
at which they all reminisce: "Do you remember the day
that . . . ?" A *tal señor, tal honor* homage is paid to the high
and mighty.

People talk about Picasso—not my father but the great Picasso. *"¡Qué talento! ¡Qué genio!"* And they drink. And they eat.
And they bawl. *Abrazos,* laughter, full mouths, grins, knowing
winks, a cacophony of voices. Harsh and grating. *Comida hecha,
compañía deshecha*—when the party's over, good-bye to the saint;
by tomorrow my father will be forgotten.

Among the mourners is one of Grandfather's nephews.
He comes up to me and whispers in my ear, "It's good that
you're alive." Paloma, Maya, Christine and her son Bernard,
my half brother and all the others, gather around me. "Marina, you must be brave." "Marina, you haven't had an easy
life." "Marina, your grandfather, your brother and now your
father. Poor little Marina." Poor little Marina. People are concerned about me. I exist in death.

The next day, I have an appointment with Maître Bacqué
de Sariac, one of my grandfather's attorneys. He wants to give
me an envelope that my father left me. It contains a hundred
thousand francs and a note in shaky handwriting: "I'm leav-

ing you this sum to help you. I hug you." It is signed "Paulo." Just "Paulo."

"Your father wanted to give it to you himself," Maître Bacqué de Sariac explains, "but he didn't dare get in touch with you." I'd like to tell him that, in any case, I wouldn't have accepted this money from my father. I'd like to tell him, but what's the point? I have no resentment now. Just an envelope containing a hundred thousand francs. Repentance in the guise of a last allowance.

Claude goes to great lengths for me. I'm a provincial. He finds it normal to be steering me around the maze of the Paris business world. "This afternoon, you'll be meeting Maître Zecri, he tells me. He is expecting you. I phoned him."

Because of my father's death, my half brother Bernard and I are now included in the Picasso estate with the same rights as Claude, Jacqueline, Maya and Paloma. Claude doesn't want trouble; he wants everything to go smoothly. "You know, we've had our share of suffering too. We had a period of adversity too. . . ." He wants to equalize our suffering, to say that we're all in the same boat—whereas I have lost Pablito.

I don't feel like replying. I don't owe anyone explanations, I have no scores to settle, I have only one thought—extracting myself from this business and escaping from this family that is held together by interests from beyond the grave.

Maître Pierre Zecri, the attorney in charge of the estate, receives me the way all attorneys receive eligible parties. "Marina Picasso, daughter of Paulo Picasso and Émilienne Lotte, his divorced wife, in compliance with the statutes of intestate cases . . ." I don't listen. I have other worries. When I walked into his office, I broke the heel of one of my clogs, and I have no other shoes to wear. My mind wanders. I don't feel concerned by all this legal talk. I'm pleased about one thing: With the money contained in the envelope that my father left me and the check that Maître Zecri has given me as an advance, I will be able to reimburse Marie-Thérèse Walter, pay the last installments on my VW and perhaps . . . nothing. I have no desire for anything.

THE FIRST THING I do on my return to Golfe-Juan is deposit the money I've just received in the bank, in my mother's account. The account is in the red, of course. Oddly enough, my mother, who has always fantasized about the Picasso wealth, does not want to take advantage of the money that she could spend any way she wants. On the contrary, she continues to economize. Her delusions have switched gears. She is no longer haunted by my grandfather's power but by her own power. "It's a good thing I'm here to administer my daughter's capital. It's a good thing she listens to me. She relies on me." The grocer, the baker, the butcher, the hardware store owner and all their customers are full of admiration. That's what's important to her.

Chapter Thirteen

When you've spent your childhood and adolescence begging for love and a bit of attention, when you've never had a cent in your pocket and borne your name like a cross, when you've owned nothing and lost everything, to receive an inheritance is like being condemned. I know what some people will say: "Her grandfather is famous, he leaves her a fortune, she has a lot of money. What is she complaining about?" I'm not complaining. I'm just trying to remember the facts as I lived them.

The first time I was invited to a discussion about the inheritance, I had no idea what was expected of me. I had only one desire—to escape from the Picasso clan. In order to do so as quickly as possible, I turned down the share that my grandmother Olga had left to my father, and Pablito's share, which normally would have been divided between me and my half brother Bernard. I didn't want any complications. I was too badly wounded. To be freer still, I had to buy up the property rights belonging to Christine, the inheritance due to her as my father's second wife. My mother wasn't entitled to even so much as a cent, but I had to make this awkward request. Very kindly—and because she knew what Pablito and I had endured—Christine accepted immediately. I was freed of the Picasso shackles.

The art expert Maurice Rheims had been given the task of estimating the thousands of works that were part of my grandfather's estate. Afterward, he and a horde of lawyers went about dividing the works into as many lots as there were heirs. Jean Leymarie and Dominique Bozo—the directors of the Picasso Museum in Paris—selected the paintings, drawings, prints and ceramics that the state was entitled to by way of inheritance taxes. Once we had paid the fees of Maître Rheims and the lawyers, Jacqueline, Maya, Paloma, Claude, Bernard and I could finally collect our inheritance.

Of course, we first had to pay our individual inheritance taxes, which in my case came to the equivalent of half the estate that my grandfather had left me. I did not want to see the spoils of my inheritance, and when the director of the Banque Nationale de Paris offered to open the doors to the vault containing my share of Picassos, I flatly refused. I didn't feel strong enough to face this final stage. Since I hated the man for the suffering that my brother and I had endured, I found it illogical for me to own anything by him. I couldn't dissociate the artist from his work.

I also inherited La Californie, with those gates that had kept us out and its oppressive rooms that smelled of the forbidden. I didn't want it. I decided to sell it and buy back my soul. I tried to get rid of it, but I couldn't find a buyer, so in the end I kept it. I couldn't make up my mind to live in it, though. I found it too large and too oppressive. I could hear the floors squeaking, the wind sweeping through the rooms. I was probably afraid of coming across the ghost—not of my grandfather, but of Picasso.

The size of La Californie frightened me, but for a long time so did anything gigantic. I remember the discomfort I felt, in the United States, when I was given an oversized glass of Coca-Cola or enormous containers of popcorn. Coke, popcorn, huge avenues, wide-open spaces, skyscrapers, American cars—even the sky there crushed me and made me black out. During my analysis, I would realize that this phobia came from my grandfather. Because of the large place he occupied in my life.

Years later—Gaël and Flore were already born—I decided to look at the collection of Picassos I'd been given. It was horrible. Though before me were treasures, I suffered a dizzy spell and had to leave the premises. Whenever I was asked to participate in an event concerning my grandfather, I couldn't bring myself to go and, when I did, my anguish was so great that I would faint.

On the advice of Jan Krugier—an art dealer, but more important, a friend to whom I had given the task of administering my collection—I had several paintings sent to the apartment in Cannes where I was living at the time. For months, they stayed turned against the walls in a room I didn't dare enter because of the unbearable anguish they caused me.

⸺

I'M OFTEN ASKED what this newly acquired wealth meant to me. What I did with it. In memory of my father, I bought a motorcycle, a Porsche and then, because he had dreamed of owning one, a Ferrari that I kept only for a short time. In memory of my grandmother Olga and her last days at the clinic where Pablito and I used to visit her, I had a fur blanket made that revived her warmth and elegance. Finally, I gave all the friends from my childhood at Golfe-Juan refrigerators, coats, fur-lined cloaks, radios, televisions, cars, probably because, at the time, we didn't own these things. Afterward, I bought a house at Cap d'Antibes, which I later gave to my mother. I certainly owed it to her. I also indulged myself. I felt I owed it to myself. Finally, I was able to help children in distress halfway around the world—my Ho Chi Minh children. I certainly owed it to them.

＊

NOW MONEY is a tool that gives me freedom, and that's all. I have a car I use to pick up my children at school, another car to take them on vacation, and a Jeep that I lend to Flore and her fiancé, Arnaud, who run a riding club in Valbonne. Though it may disappoint the people who think I live like a billionaire, I don't own a Mediterranean yacht and I have never rented a private plane for my trips. I don't stay in luxury hotels or go to trendy clubs where people go to be seen, or to tea rooms for ladies of leisure. I'm not a member of the jet set. Out of decency, I've always refused child benefits, and so as not to take advantage of the free government health program, I've taken out private insurance for my children and me. I can at least show that much propriety, that much respect. But here again, I'll leave a blank. I don't like talking about money. Perhaps because I have some. Or because I didn't have any when we lived in the shadow of a genius.

Chapter Fourteen

The word "genius," which Picasso experts love to use, annoys me and makes me indignant. I don't understand how they can analyze his work in a redundant, pompous jargon aimed at a small group of initiates: "the Hispanic mobility of the reds and yellowish browns," "the cosmic impulse of the line," "the composition's chimerical problematic." How dare they presume to lock Picasso and his oeuvre inside a fortress whose key they alone possess?

Picasso and genius, genius and Picasso: two inseparable

words that are useful for dinner parties. "Picasso's terrific. Pure, unadulterated genius! Please help yourself to some more asparagus. It comes from our property in Provence."

And the comments overheard in bars: "A genius. A genius. If I were Picasso, given the price of his paintings, I'd paint one and stop right there."

The Picasso name—the name I bear—has become a trademark. It's in the shop windows of perfume and jewelry stores, on ashtrays, neckties and T-shirts. You can't turn on the television without seeing a robot airbrushing the signature Picasso on the side of a car. Not to mention the Picasso Administration, the enterprise that manages the Picasso empire, which I refused to be a part of.

Picasso, that forbidden grandfather whom I always saw wearing espadrilles, old shorts and an undershirt with holes, that Spaniard who was much more of an Anarchist than a Communist, could never have imagined that—outside his painting—his name would one day become a moneymaking machine.

After fourteen years of analysis, I've come to realize the extent to which the image I had of my grandfather was distorted, frightening and alarming. Through the prism of my father, he was contemptuous and stingy; through that of my mother, he was perverse and insensitive. Jacqueline, referring to him as "Monseigneur," dealt us the crowning blow: Through her, we saw him as one of those cruel gods to whom the Aztecs offered human sacrifices.

Brought up on this myth, for a long time I thought that he alone was responsible for our misery. Everything was his fault: my father's failure, my mother's excesses, my grandmother Olga's decline, my brother Pablito's depression and death. I resented him for never thinking about our fate and for abandoning us. I couldn't understand why Pablito and I couldn't see him alone. I couldn't understand why he wasn't interested in his grandchildren when we demanded no more than a tiny drop of interest.

Now—and here is one of the reasons for this book—I've discovered that our grandfather was stolen from us. Pablito and I may have casually slipped into his life, but the irresponsibility of father, mother and possessive wife stripped us of the affection that Pablito and I craved every time we visited him.

Shuttered in an atmosphere of such servility, how could it occur to that living god that, behind each of our visits to La Californie, there was a cry for help? It would have been enough for Picasso to descend from his Mount Olympus for just a few minutes and, for the duration of a caress, become a grandfather like any other. He couldn't. Isolated inside his oeuvre, he had lost all contact with reality and withdrawn into an impenetrable inner world.

This oeuvre was his only language, his only vision of the world. Even as a child, he had already been shut inside himself. In school, in Málaga, while the other pupils listened to the teacher, he used to draw pigeons and bullfights tirelessly in his notebooks. When his teachers reprimanded him, he used to scoff at them. His drawings were as good as all the courses in arithmetic, Spanish and history.

He was insatiable and devoured life, people and things. A stone, a piece of wood or tile, a fragment of crockery—each became creations in his hands. In the morning, he went jogging. He would tail the car, driven by Jacqueline. Along the way, he would throw onto the back seat a bit of scrap iron, a bicycle seat or handlebars, whatever he found in the trash cans lining the route. When he worked on them in his studio, the scrap iron, seat or handlebars were transformed into an owl, an African mask or a Minotaur.

For Picasso, the most banal object became a work of art.

The same was true of the women who had the privilege— or misfortune—of being swept up in his tornado. He submitted them to his animal sexuality, tamed them, bewitched them, ingested them and crushed them onto his canvas. After he had spent many nights extracting their essence, once they were bled dry, he would dispose of them.

His magnetic gaze was like a scalpel; he would dig into reality, work on it and carve it up. With his brush and hands, he overpowered colors, clay, bronze, metal. He subdued women and inert matter and made them his slaves.

Though his life spanned most of the twentieth century, he didn't live like his contemporaries. In fact, he didn't see them. His life was a sketchbook, a book of images roughed out in the course of his dazzling creativity.

He didn't re-create the world; he imposed his own.

Throughout his life, in every period in his painting, he sought to track down the ephemeral and capture the moment. He wasn't painting, he wasn't drawing, he wasn't sculpting, he was pouring out everything he felt. He was dissecting his soul. Modesty and immodesty, vitality and death, violence and sensitivity, provocation and naiveté, he made all those strings vibrate with such intensity that it electrified everyone who came near him. And struck them down.

He was merciless in this quest for the absolute. He didn't care what weapons he used. Like Don Quixote, he was under the compulsion to fight and wreak revenge on a world that he wanted to master.

"A good painting," he used to say, "must be spiked with razor blades."

This little man, barely five-foot-three, was, like the title of his famous self-portrait, *Yo Picasso.* Like the dazzling matador standing in the sandy arena, his only fear was death. His sword was a paintbrush, his *muleta* a virgin canvas.

None of us—not my father, my mother, Pablito or I—could understand the isolation in which this matador was struggling. No one had access to his bullfight—his eternal crusade.

Who were we to think we could violate the arena in which he fought? What impudence to request of this man all the things that he had given up so he could dedicate himself to his art—money, family, tenderness, consideration. Those thousands of trivial things that are part of the everyday life of traditional families.

How can we reproach him for not seeing that we were children, Pablito and I? Childhood, like everything else, couldn't be anything other than his creation.

"At eight, I was Raphael," he used to say. "It took me a whole lifetime to paint like a child."

We were his rivals.

The usual gamut of feelings had no hold at all over him. He liked money in order to buy houses in which he could paint. He would sell them as soon as they were too small to contain his new works. He didn't like to sit down at the table for a meal. This was time stolen from his creation. He had contempt for all the superficial things that money could buy. In his used clothes he could have been mistaken for a bum. He set no store by the court that crowded to see the master— his "frog pond," as he called it.

By the end of his life he had turned everyone away so he could be alone and use his last remaining strength to create. We were among those he had turned away.

Thanks to analysis, I've been able to discover a grandfather that I didn't know. I used to wait for him to open the gate behind which he had taken refuge. Perhaps he wanted to open it. I'll never know. Perhaps by the time he wanted to open the gate, it was too heavy, and he was too tired.

In the end, who was more egotistical, Picasso or me?

ISOLATED inside Notre-Dame-de-Vie, he died in the same way as he had lived: alone, which is how he had wanted to be.

He had made this cruel statement: "When I die, it will be a shipwreck. When a large ship goes down many people in the vicinity are swept into the whirlpool."

It's true, many people were swept into the whirlpool.

Pablito, my inseparable brother, committed suicide two days after our grandfather was buried at Vauvenargues.

My father, the frail giant, died two years later feeling desperately orphaned.

Marie-Thérèse Walter, the inconsolable muse, hanged herself from the ceiling in her garage in Juan-les-Pins.

Jacqueline, the companion of his last days, also committed suicide with a bullet in her temple.

Later, Dora Maar died in poverty surrounded by the Picasso paintings she had refused to sell, so she could preserve for herself the presence of the man whom she idolized.

I was meant to be one of the victims as well. If I'm still around, I owe it to a lust for life and struggle, which I inherited from a grandfather I dreamed about. And who wasn't there.

Chapter Fifteen

Now I've put down my bag, like a sailor who has been sailing the seven seas for a lifetime. I don't want it weighing down on my shoulder anymore. It's much too heavy—too heavy and too shabby.

I'm sitting—not lying down anymore—in my analyst's office, and I can finally take my fate into my own hands.

I'm Marina Picasso.

"That's good," the analyst answers simply.

He understands that I'm ready to turn a page—turn a page on pain.

The most important things in my life now are my children, Gaël and Flore, to whom I was unable to completely devote myself during my "dark years." I want to find them again, get to know them, help them to get to know me, gently, step by step, like a convalescent.

Together we travel and discover the world—China, Africa, Russia. The sights make a striking impression on us and bring us closer, unite us and bind us. The happiness they feel and the happiness they give me sharpen my maternal feelings. As I gradually rediscover the world, I feel a desire to have more children. Gaël and Flore applaud the idea. They too want to enlarge the family with brothers and sisters.

"What about adopting?" they ask.

"I'd like to—if you agree."

"Yes, we agree!"

We've just sealed a pact.

MONIQUE, the guide at the Kuoni travel agency who organized every one of our trips, comes to dinner with a Vietnamese friend. Her friend François was educated in France and has always maintained close ties with his country. Encouraged by his kindness and his passion when he talks about Vietnam, I tell him about my plan to adopt children. He listens to me, sounds me out and explains—after what might have been construed as a cross-examination—that he thinks I would have no difficulty in adopting a Vietnamese child.

"There are so many children seeking a family. There are so many who are dying."

He knows a physician in Ho Chi Minh City, at Grall Children's Hospital, a former French military hospital. He will talk to her about me.

"Who is she?"

"Madame Hoa has used part of her wealth to help the underprivileged children of Ho Chi Minh City. She was Minister of Health for many years. Today she works in research and tries to improve the living conditions of the girls and boys under her care in the hospital."

"When can I see her?"

"I'm leaving in a few days. As soon as I return, I'll get in touch with you."

All I have to do is wait.

MADAME HOA is expecting us, Gaël, Flore and me. When François told her of my request, she quickly made all the necessary arrangements to help me. She has found a baby for me.

Like François, Madame Hoa was educated in Paris. As fate would have it—coincidence or destiny?—she knew my grandfather in the 1950s. They belonged to the same Communist Party cell in the Eighteenth Arrondissement of Paris.

We arrive at the airport in Ho Chi Minh City and deal with the hassle of customs. Gaël and Flore's excitement and my own impatience are palpable. Soon, I'll be holding in my arms the child I want so badly, the child of my resurrection.

His name will be Florian.

As we ride in the minibus that has come to pick us up, we discover the streets, the picturesque houses, the artisans' stalls, the bustling crowd, the colors, the fragrance of spice, of musk, of mugginess. The fragrance of paradise. At the far end of the city, a baby is waiting for us.

But, when we arrive, the Grall Hospital nursery has just locked its doors. We'll have to come back in the morning to get acquainted with Florian. I'm disappointed. The night is endless when you've lived for so long on hopes and on a trust that is usually disappointed.

The next morning, we are let in to the nursery. Florian is here, scrawny and tiny. Dr. Hoa had arranged for him to come from the Go Vap orphanage so she could care for him before entrusting him to me. His limbs are emaciated. Like all children who have suffered from malnutrition, his stomach is bloated. He's only three months old but he has a lively look in his eyes.

"Picasso's eyes," Madame Hoa says to me in a whisper.

I smile.

I still have a few days left before returning to France with Florian in my arms. In the meantime, Madame Hoa offers to take me to visit several orphanages and hospitals that she's in charge of. She tells me that in Ho Chi Minh City alone, it is estimated that 21,000 children have been abandoned and have to fend for themselves on the streets. Only fifteen hundred were counted in the census.

Wretched orphanages, hospitals and hospices where children, elderly people and sick people are crowded together. Because of poverty and a lack of funds, the hygienic conditions are dreadful. My heart bleeds. I must do something and I have so little time.

⟡

I CONTACT the People's Committee, the Communist Party leaders, the Social Services. I move heaven and earth. This country has given me a child; it is my duty to help it. My name pleads in my favor. As the granddaughter of Comrade Picasso, the people I contact listen to me and encourage me. They agree to take part in my humanitarian action.

The head of the Social Services in charge of health problems in the south of the country offers to show me land in Thu Duc, in the northern suburbs of Ho Chi Minh City. He knows that I want to build a village for unfortunate children. I don't yet know how I'll go about it, but I want my wealth to serve a purpose. I'm not Mother Teresa, but the suffering of the orphans that I witnessed in the institutions I visited with Madame Hoa has become intolerable to me. I must throw myself into this completely and do everything possible for them.

Thu Duc is a former military area of five thousand square meters covered with marshes, water holes caused by the monsoons, and a subtropical, chaotic vegetation—mangrove swamps, bamboo undergrowth, palm trees run wild. On the edge of the land sits a dilapidated building with peeling walls, eroded by saltpeter.

At my request, the head of the Social Services takes me around. In front of the door, there are orphans playing ball like children everywhere in the world. Inside, all alone in a large room, a small boy in striped pajamas looks at me. He's balding, his face is emaciated and his eyes are sad and poignant. He knows he will die of the cancer that is devastating him. He's only eight years old.

The decision is made; with the agreement of the Vietnamese authorities, Thu Duc will become "The Village of Youth."

That this village exists today is thanks to Florian, the little boy in striped pajamas and especially my brother, Pablito. The three hundred fifty children who can live a dignified life there owe it to them. Memories and the expressions in a child's eyes can perform miracles.

On the return flight, Florian is curled up in my arms and I hold him tightly against me. He is grasping Gaël's index finger in his right hand and Flore's pinky in his left. From the windows in the plane, we see the sky spotted with clouds.

WE RETURN to Cannes and La Californie, where the doors are wide open to welcome Florian. La Californie, where laughter rings out in every room. La Californie, now the scene of a childhood that should have been mine and Pablito's— a childhood full of concern, care and attentiveness.

"What time does baby wake up?"

"When are you giving baby his bath?"

"Did you remember baby's bottle?"

The word "baby" that Gaël and Flore are bubbling over with as they look down into Florian's crib invigorates and stimulates me. More babies are waiting for me in Vietnam. I must act fast.

Between two visits to Lenval Hospital, where I have Florian examined, I see the architect who renovated La Californie for me. I hand him the plans that the Vietnamese authorities have given me so that he can draw up the plans for the Village of Youth in collaboration with an architect from Ho Chi Minh City. I don't want buildings resembling barracks in Thu Duc; I want him to build little houses that will each have a kitchen, a bathroom, a dining room and bed-rooms. I also want a school, a gymnasium, a stadium, a swim-ming pool, a park. I want the children who will live there to find a family, and the love they didn't have.

That's the least that life owes them.

—

I RETURN to Vietnam, where destiny guides me. Once again, Gaël and Flore are here to help me shape it. We have agreed among us to adopt other little children. And, if I were to listen to them, many little children. "Babies," as they say.

At the airport in Ho Chi Minh City, a red carpet has been spread out at the foot of the gangway and, under the red flag with a yellow star, the highest dignitaries of the country are waiting for me. It is not me that they have come to honor but my grandfather, the father of the Dove and of *Guernica*.

"Comrade Picasso, did you have a good trip?"

"Comrade Picasso, this country is yours."

I'm a native child of this land.

While the architects and workers begin their efforts at the construction site that will become, six months later, the first segment of the Village of Youth, I am greeted by Madame Hoa at Grall Hospital. Waiting for me here is May, a one-and-a-half-year-old. Like Florian, she comes from the Go Vap orphanage. Like him, she is seriously malnourished. The only people she's familiar with are the nurses and staff at Go Vap and Grall Hospital. May won't let me get near her; she refuses to come out of her cocoon. She struggles and screams. I must be careful not to rush her. I know it will be difficult to cut her roots, roots that since birth have been nourished on misfortune, the only sap she knows.

My life is divided between Vietnam and Europe. In 1990 the Village of Youth is completed, but I still want to develop its reception facilities and buy the neighboring military land. Construction starts again with the same energy, the same faith. At the same time, my foundation arranges for regular shipments of several tons of milk for the children in the orphanages and hospitals of Ho Chi Minh City; it organizes the digging of artesian wells in the inland villages. It grants a subsidy to a village of retired people and veterans so that they can raise livestock and begin farming, and it gives scholarship help to two hundred students at the University of Da Lat, northeast of Ho Chi Minh City.

Because of the poor state of the children's hospitals and their inadequate medical equipment, my foundation, with subsidies from France, supports the renovation of two pediatric hospitals in the capital and finances the creation of surgical and intensive care units. Furthermore, I decide to pay tribute to Madame Hoa by modernizing the Go Vap orphanage, which had been a home to Florian and May. With the consent of the authorities, improvements are made inside;

it is repainted and given new furniture. Seamstresses are hired to make clothes for the young boarders. Covered playgrounds are built so the children can play during the rainy season.

I follow my instincts, and do what I feel I must do. I don't calculate. I deal with the most urgent matters first.

As Picasso used to say, I don't seek, I find.

—

I MAKE ANOTHER TRIP to Ho Chi Minh City with Gaël, Flore and two-and-a-half-year-old May. Florian, twenty months old, has stayed in France. We've come for another child, from an orphanage run by the charity Terre des Hommes.

As soon as I see fifteen-month-old Dimitri, I know he is the one—the new child who will join our family. Abandoned when he was only three days old, Dimitri knows nothing of the world. Every little thing seems to fascinate him—a bird flying past a window, a gust of wind blowing through a tree, the sound of a faraway car. Finger pointing up, he marvels at these minor miracles, and his exclamations of wonder—"Oh!"—are such tender music to my ears that I had to adopt him. I have him examined at the Carpentier Foundation in Saigon, and then take him home with great pomp. He has not yet learned to walk; he prefers to hang on to me, like a drowning person clings to a life preserver. "Your arms . . . your arms"—these are the only words he rewards me with for many months to come. Arms that are wide open for him.

—

That's my life. Invited to its banquet, I've done what I could and what I thought I had to do. Sometimes good, sometimes bad.

"When I don't have any blue, I use red," my grandfather used to say.

I have had to use the colors offered me by fate. Some were primary, others complementary. Tints and half-tints. I hope my children will not pass judgment on my life.

Now that I've crossed the Rubicon, I have a new way of looking at things, one I didn't have when I was bringing up Gaël and Flore. I had a desperate and passionate love for them, a love that was timeless and animal-like.

I try to give my adopted children, May, Dimitri and Florian, a love that will help them, first of all, to shape their own identity. I'm there every morning, before they go to school, to make sure they've brushed their teeth, put on good shoes and dressed warmly. I make them eat breakfast, quiz them on their schoolwork, and check their schoolbags or knapsacks.

Gaël telephones me from London. He's expecting me next week.

Flore and Arnaud are stopping by tomorrow after having tended to their horses at the Mougins riding school.

Florian, eleven and a half, is at his judo class. This morning he told me about his plans for the future. He's going to be a cook, and if that doesn't work out, the head of a platoon in the national police force.

May, who is twelve, wants to be a French teacher or a movie star.

Dimitri, who is eleven, wants to be an airline pilot but also an architect on the days when Air France is on strike.

It's five in the evening. The sun is setting over the Îles de Lérins.

I'm at peace with myself.

MARINA PICASSO is the founder of several charitable organizations that help underprivileged children in Vietnam. The mother of five, including three adopted Vietnamese children, she lives in the villa in the South of France that she inherited from her grandfather.